DEVELOPING MENTAL MATHS

WITH 5-7 YEAR OLDS

ROS LEATHER

Published by Scholastic Ltd
Villiers House
Clarendon Avenue
Leamington Spa
Warwickshire CV32 5PR

Text © 1997 Ros Leather
© 1997 Scholastic Ltd

567890   90123456

AUTHOR
Ros Leather

SERIES CONSULTANT
Tamara Bibby

EDITOR
Kate Pearce

ASSISTANT EDITOR
Lesley Sudlow

SERIES DESIGNER
Anna Oliwa

DESIGNER
Louise Belcher

ILLUSTRATIONS
Nick Diggory

COVER ARTWORK
James Alexander/David Oliver
(Berkeley Studios)

Designed using Aldus Pagemaker

British Library Cataloguing-in-Publication Data
A catalogue record for this book is available from the British
Library.

ISBN 0-590-53763-6

CONTENTS

Mathematics does not exist in the world independent of the people who use it. It exists primarily in people's heads and is, therefore, a mental activity.

Many adults in Britain today remember learning maths in primary school as a repetitive cycle of the teacher demonstrating a method and working through an example on the board, then setting a page of practice 'sums' to reinforce that method. These methods, or algorithms, many of which we still use, were developed so that the clerks and shopkeepers of post-Industrial Revolution Europe could accurately add and subtract, multiply and divide long columns of numbers.

We no longer need to work in that way – the mathematical demands of modern society are very different. We need to be able to read, and make sense of, a much wider range of numerical information – statistics including interest rates and other variable percentages and ratios, as well as the vast array of graphs and charts that have accompanied the computer revolution. Simply being able to apply the four rules of number in a narrow range of situations is no longer adequate.

BECOMING NUMERATE

We need to broaden our perception of numeracy just as we have had to broaden our concept of what it means to be literate. The mathematics taught in primary schools should help pupils to become truly numerate, giving them an ability, and a willingness, to use mathematical skills and tools to tackle numerical problems in flexible and creative ways. A mechanical training in performing basic skills and operations is not enough.

Pupils need to be able to use mathematical skills and tools with equal facility in a wide range of contexts. People who are numerate are able to:
● perform number operations with measures and money as well as out of context (as pages of 'sums');
● deal with numerical information presented in a variety of ways including diagrams, graphs, tables and charts;
● make decisions about whether to work mentally, on paper, or with a calculator depending on the degree of accuracy needed and the complexity of the task.

THE IMPORTANCE OF MENTAL CALCULATION

Over a period of many years Her Majesty's Inspectors have called for increased attention to be given to mental calculation. They have highlighted an over-reliance on counting methods among older KS2 children, as well as an inability to make sensible estimates (HMCI Annual Report 1994/95, for example). Suggestions have been made that teachers need to help children to develop their mathematical language skills as well as a 'feel for number' by using discussion to challenge their understanding. Further emphasis has been placed upon the importance of identifying, analysing and correcting errors and misconceptions in the understanding of number (*The Teaching and Learning of Number in Primary Schools, Mathematics AT2*, 1993).

Recently, the Government became so concerned over the apparent drop in standards in numeracy that they set up twelve national centres to work with schools and teachers to raise standards of attainment (the National Numeracy Project). The Government's concern over standards in numeracy has been echoed by public concern and repeated calls for a return to the teaching of mental maths. These concerns are not new, and were particularly well articulated in the Cockcroft Report (1982).

Many of the points that Cockcroft made continue to be repeated in the public debate today:

255 *We believe that the decline of mental and oral work within mathematics classrooms represents a failure to recognise the central place which working 'done in the head' occupies throughout mathematics. Even when using traditional methods of recording calculations on paper, the written record is usually based on steps which are done mentally.*

When working on 'everyday maths' people who are 'mathematically effective' do not use the standard written methods they were taught in school, they work mentally and use personal methods.

The Cockcroft Report pointed out that:

256 *Although many pupils come to realise by themselves that methods which may be convenient on paper are often not well suited to use 'in their heads', we believe that in the case of many other pupils it is necessary for the teacher to point out explicitly and to discuss at length the variety of methods which it is possible to use...*

Although many people do develop flexible methods on their own this has generally been achieved in spite of the teaching they received – the development of a range of flexible methods is rarely explicitly encouraged. Teachers cannot trust to luck – pupils need to be taught to develop a variety of flexible methods which can be used appropriately in different contexts. However, as Cockcroft goes on to say:

> ... no attempt should be made to force a single 'proper method' of performing mental calculations; pupils should be encouraged to make use of whatever methods suit them best. Teachers should also encourage pupils to reflect upon the methods which they develop for themselves so that facility in mental computation can be consolidated and extended.

The Mathematics National Curriculum (1995) states that:

> pupils should be given opportunities to develop flexible methods of working with number, orally and mentally.
> (KS1 Number 1a)

> pupils should be given opportunities to develop flexible methods of computation and recording, and use them with understanding; and develop the skills needed for accurate and appropriate use of equipment. (KS2 Number 1a and c)

and, more specifically:

> pupils should be taught to develop a variety of mental methods of computation with whole numbers to 100, and explain patterns used; extend mental methods to develop a range of non-calculator methods of computation that involve addition and subtraction of whole numbers, progressing to methods for multiplication and division of up to three-digit by two-digit whole numbers.
> (KS2 Number 3d)

The Scottish Guidelines for Mathematics 5–14 considers 'using mental methods' as a discrete issue in maths teaching, exemplifying the range of methods that might be used for straightforward mental calculation and going on to state that:

> It is important, then, to recognise that when calculating mentally we usually make use of different methods from those

we have used for written calculations. We should encourage pupils to develop and practise flexible mental approaches. One way of doing this is through class or group discussion of the different ways of carrying out particular calculations.

With regard to school schemes of work, the non-statutory guidance of the National Curriculum (1989) states that:

511 Activities should encourage pupils to use mental arithmetic and to become confident in the use of a range of mathematical tools.
● The ability to use mental arithmetic in everyday life and work is very important. This includes the vital skills of estimating results in advance, and of checking answers mentally for accuracy and reasonableness.
● Activities should provide opportunities for pupils to develop skills in selecting and using a wide range of mathematical tools – constructional kits, drawing instruments, measuring equipment, calculating aids, electronic calculators and micro-computers. They should also help pupils to select with confidence the most appropriate ways to tackle different problems.

BUILDING UP MENTAL IMAGES

For children to develop effective mental strategies they need strong mental images of the number system. They also need to see – and be able to show – how the mathematics can be explained.

There are many resources available which can be used to help children develop strong mental images of the number system. The most easily

available (and the cheapest) are children's fingers. Fingers are particularly useful for seeing the number pairs that make 5 or 10 (1 + 4, 2 + 3, 3 + 2, 4 + 1 and 1 + 9, 2 + 8 and so on).

The number line is a resource which helps children develop a sense of the structure of the number system beyond ten. A number line, preferably to 120, with each decade demarcated with a different colour or shape, will provide children with a visual reminder to confirm their oral counting. Such a resource also shows how our numbers change and repeat; children should be helped to observe how the 10s number increases by 1 after a 9 and that the numbers 0 to 9 all come in turn to make a decade.

A visual aid such as a number line or hundred square also helps to bring some order into our spoken numbers which can be extremely confusing to young children. The teen numbers are especially problematic; when we say 13, for example, the first sound is 'th' and many children, therefore, assume that it should begin with the number 3. In the early years at school, children will need to be taught, and have ample opportunity to practise, diverse methods of counting. This will enable them to become confident, creative and to have the ability to combine methods when problem solving.

DEVELOPING COUNTING

Once the children are counting on and back in strings efficiently from any number they can begin to move from a 'count all' strategy to the more efficient 'counting on' strategy. There are several ways to model counting on:
● to work out 6 + 3 with objects count out the two groups and keep them separate, confirm that

there are 6 in the first group and place a hand on them and say six, then count on three more;
● along the number line, for example, counting on from a number saying '6, 7, 8, 9';
● by putting a number in your head and counting on. Place your hand on your head and say 6, hold up 3 fingers and count 7, 8, 9 as the fingers are unfolded.

There are two methods of subtraction which need to be modelled:
● counting on from the small number to the larger number; this is referred to as the 'Shop-keeper's method' as it is similar to giving change. This method is often used when finding the difference;
● counting back from the large number to the small number.

Counting in 2s, 5s and 10s is a skill which we value – it enables us to count large groups of objects more efficiently. However, to many children the act of counting in groups lacks purpose. The use of 'pregrouped' objects such as hands (5 fingers), feet, as well as 2p, 5p, and 10p coins can help give meaning to the uses of counting in groups. Counting grouped objects or 2p, 5p or 10p coins will help children to become familiar with counting on in groups (pre-multiplication) and counting back in groups (pre-division).

It is useful to mark a number line or 0–99 square with self-adhesive notes or pegs to record the count (of 5s for example). This can help children to see the repeating patterns that are being generated. Finding and using patterns will help the children to be more efficient and adaptable when solving mathematical problems.

A demonstration of the efficiency of counting in groups can be given by asking four people to count together to 100 – four people all start counting together and each say a number word at the same time. Person one counts in 1s, person two in 2s, person three in 5s and person four in 10s.

FACT OR FIGURING OUT?

Recent research[*] points to that fact that 'knowing by heart' and 'figuring out' support each other. Working successfully in your head involves using things that you already know to derive new information. In time, the things that you used to have to work out are added to the repertoire of things that you know. As your bank of known facts increases it adds to the ways available to you to work things out.

Children in the early years should be encouraged, through activities and experience, to commit a range of number facts to memory so that they can move on to figuring out those they do not know from those they do. Further, they need to be encouraged to learn addition and subtraction facts together and multiplication and division facts together. This helps children to realise

not only that these are inverse operations, but also that if they know one fact then they also know several others. For example, if I know:

> 4 + 6 = 10 then I also know 6 + 4 = 10,
> 10 − 4 = 6 and 10 − 6 = 4
> 7 × 2 = 14 then I also know 2 × 7 = 14,
> 14 ÷ 2 = 7 and 14 ÷ 7 = 2
> double 8 is 16 so half of 16 is 8

A full range of the things children should know by the end of Year 2/Primary 3 is given in the sections at the start of each chapter in this book (pages 10–11, 30–31, 46–47 and 56–57).

To illustrate how known facts can be utilised, consider, for example:

● number bonds up to 10:

> 1 + 9 = 10   10 − 1 = 9
> 2 + 8 = 10   10 − 2 = 8 etc.

This knowledge can be adapted for different situations, for example in developing bonds to 20, or as part of a compensation strategy:

> 19 + 1 = 20   20 − 1 = 19

● doubling and halving:

The children will need to be able to double and halve all the numbers to 10. This skill can be adapted for larger numbers and 'nearly' doubles, for example:

> 30 + 30 = 60 so 30 + 29 = 59

● the patterns for counting on and back in 10s

> 6, 16, 26... 46. 36, 26...:

This will help children develop strategies for adding and subtracting 9 and 11 as well as for adding and subtracting multiples of 10. For example 33 − 9 can be worked out as 33 − 10 + 1 because you've taken away one too many, and 25 + 40 can be worked out by counting on four tens – '25, 35, 45, 55, 65'.

The following scenarios demonstrate how known facts and established strategies have been used by young children to support their problem-solving:
1. A group of 36 children had estimated and then used their knowledge of counting in 2s to work out that there were a total of 72 legs in the circle. Alex wondered how many legs and arms there were; 'It will be more than 100', he said, 'because

50 + 50 = 100.' Several children wanted to count, but Alex sat quietly. Suddenly his hand shot up, 'I know, it's 144'. He went on to explain 'because 20 + 20 = 40 and 2 + 2 = 4 – that makes 144.' The rest of the class then counted or used counting on and partitioning (70 count on 70 is 140 + 4 = 144) to verify his calculation.
2. The home corner was set up as a baker's shop and the class were posed the following shopping problem: 'A loaf of bread costs 24p today. How many loaves can you buy for £1?'

Robert looked at his £1 coin and said, 'If the bread cost 20p I could buy exactly five loaves, but it costs more – so I think it will be four loaves.' He worked out that four 20s = 80p, four 4s = 16p and 80 + 16 = 96p, so his change was 4p.

James, however, put four loaves on the table and wrote 25p on a piece of paper under each because 'there are four 25ps in a £1.' He crossed out the 25s and wrote 24s. He counted back 1 for each loaf and said, 'I can buy four loaves, they will cost 96p and I shall have 4p change!'

Most of the children needed to place money under each loaf. They needed the reassurance that the practical situation gave them. This method required the careful exchange of coins.
3. Rosie was calculating the total cost of four sweets. She wanted to solve the problem without using coins, so she put the sweets on to her book and wrote down the prices. (Three sweets cost 7p and one cost 8p.) She counted 5, 10, 15, 20, touching the 7s and 8 one at a time as she counted. She then returned to the first 7 and touched each number again, saying: '22, 24, 26, 29.' Rosie explained that she was visualising coins as she counted (5ps, then 2ps and a 1p).

Several children wanted to interrupt, but they were dissuaded. Their preferred methods were discussed later ('7 and 7 is 14, and another 7 is 21, and 8 is 29' or '7 + 7 = 14, 7 + 8 = 15; 14 + 10 = 24, and 5 is 29').

It is essential to give children time when they are working as it is easy to impose your own thinking by interrupting too quickly. Children do not all develop at the same rate and it is vital to value different models of working. Praise and encouragement, together with discussion and careful modelling, should foster positive attitudes to learning. It is important to create an, 'I can solve this problem' attitude with all our pupils. This will require sensitive handling by adults and peers. All the children should feel safe and secure in the knowledge that their ideas are valued and encouraged.

STARTING TO USE DISCUSSION

Evidence of pupils' methods of working on mental maths can only be gathered through discussion. It should be noted, however, that there is a significant difference between what may be termed 'question-and-answer sessions' and true 'discussion'. Discussion is more open and allows all participants the right to contribute. It is facilitated by the use of open (rather than closed) questions. For example, 'How many pairs of numbers can you find which add up to give 12?' is more challenging than 'What is 3 + 9?' (and demonstrates the difference between an open and a closed question). Questioning which challenges pupils to apply, synthesise or explain their knowledge is much more effective in raising attainment than questioning that merely tests the ability to recall facts and procedures.

Children in the early years are generally keen to explain how they have solved a problem. Occasionally they may say, 'I just know'. This should be accepted and praised; knowing is more efficient and effective than working it out.

While accuracy is important you can often learn more about a pupil's understanding by discussing incorrect answers. Often teachers avoid doing this because they do not want to deflate or worry a child. However, leaving a pupil knowing they 'got it wrong' can start to build an 'I can't do it' attitude which can be difficult to break later.

Fostering and encouraging these responses is vital in promoting confident, articulate and flexible thinking in mathematics. Each activity in this book offers specific questions to help you draw out the maths from the children. Where it is appropriate, ways of introducing specific mathematical language and the correct vocabulary are highlighted.

Although at all times you need to guard against turning a mental strategy into another algorithm to learn, it may be necessary to offer a more efficient strategy if it is not being developed by the children. Any strategies that you offer in this spirit need to be added to the range of strategies available rather than being offered to replace the others.

WAIT TIME

The time between asking a question and expecting a response is called 'wait time'. Research[*] has shown that many teachers wait for less than one second before expecting a pupil to answer or moving on to someone else. A wait time of about three seconds significantly improves both the achievement and attitudes of pupils. But getting the wait time right is important. Perhaps surprisingly, waiting too long for an answer can have the effect of decreasing the quality of interaction between teacher and pupil and reducing the level of pupil achievement.

When thinking about how much wait time to leave, it is important to consider the kind of question you have asked – a test of quick recall requires a shorter wait time than a more challenging question; a single word reply takes less time to formulate than an explanation or a description.

THE USE OF PRAISE

Praise is important. We praise positive behaviours to reinforce them, but to be really effective praise needs to be specific. 'Good' and 'Well done' are vague – what was good? Which bit of what I just did, did I do well?

'Well done, you remembered that it is quicker to count on from the largest number. That is much more efficient, isn't it?';

'Good, you remembered the pattern of counting on in 10s without adding on ten 1s' are specific – the child is left in no doubt as to what was done well, the positive has been reinforced.

Even where incorrect answers have been reached, praise can be used to boost children's confidence and self-esteem; 'You were nearly right, the strategy was a good one and it would have worked if you had remembered to add on the extra number.'

DISCUSSION DEVICES

Managing discussions is difficult – especially if you and your class are new to the idea. Here are some things you might find useful to try:

● count to 5 in your head before expecting an answer;

● let the children know you are going to ask lots of people what they think before you all discuss their responses;

● don't let pupils put their hands up, but put their thumb on their laps instead;

● supply paper and pencils and ask the children to jot down their answers;

● you may like the youngest children to know that you will be going round the circle giving everyone a turn;

● pose a problem to be worked out in pairs.

Before the pupils report back, give them a time warning: 'In three minutes we are going to hear what everyone has found out. You need to decide who is going to report back and what they are going to say':

● encourage pupils to think carefully before they respond;

● encourage pupils to develop a clear style of explanation.

GENERIC QUESTIONS

There are many questions which are generally useful in this type of discussion and some of these are listed below. They may be useful as starting points for discussion about any of the activities in this book. (In addition, each activity in this book has some specific questions suggested alongside.)

What answer did you get?
How did you do that?
Did anyone else use that method?
Did anyone get the same answer by a different method?
Did anyone get a different answer?
How did you get that answer?
Were there any other answers or methods?
Do you think we can have more than one correct answer for this problem?
Why do you think that?
Does any one disagree? (Why do you disagree?)

Which answer do we think is correct?
Why is the other answer incorrect?
Which of the methods we used is the most efficient? Why?
Who used that method? (A number of hands go up.) Good.
Who thinks they could try that method for this problem?

FOLLOW-UP

● Have a 'Fact of the day' and return to it frequently throughout the day.

● Ask children how they are going to remember in future.

● Ask children what mistake they made and how they will remember not to make it again.

● Ask other children how they might help an individual remember something.

● Ask children to invent mnemonics.

THE ACTIVITIES IN THIS BOOK

The activities in this book are organised into four sections:

● Counting and ordering numbers.
● Addition and subtraction.
● Multiplication and division.
● Multistep and mixed operations.

Each section starts with examples of the kinds of strategies that need to be developed by Reception and Years 1 and 2/P1–3 in Scotland and Northern Ireland. All of the activities that follow can be used as the basis for whole class or group discussions. The activities fall into four categories which reflect decreasing teacher input:

1 Teacher-directed activities: these are designed to be led exclusively by the teacher with a larger group or whole class. They focus explicitly on numbers to enable strategies to be discussed. They may be used as assessment activities.

2 Problems: these focus on number in context. The strategies will need to be applied. They may be teacher-directed or worked on collaboratively by small groups or pairs of children.

3 Investigations: these focus on number and algebra, and are designed to encourage pupils to generalise their findings.

4 Games: these are designed to be used by pairs or small groups of pupils independently. They aim to help pupils develop strategies in a less formal context.

FURTHER READING

*Askew, M. & Wiliam, D. (1995) *Recent Research in Mathematics Education 5–16*, HMSO
Merttens, R. (Ed.) *1996 Primary Professional Bookshelf: Teaching Numeracy – maths in the primary classroom*, Scholastic

DEVELOPING MENTAL MATHS

STRATEGIES

CHILDREN SHOULD BE WORKING WITH NUMBERS OF THE ORDER:

RECEPTION/PRIMARY 1

Counting:
- say the counting words as an unbreakable string to at least 10;
- count back in the context of rhymes or songs;
- accurately count a set of at least ten objects;
- say which number name comes before or after another.

Reading and ordering:
- distinguish between letters and numerals;
- know that numbers can represent a quantity (cardinality) and a position in a line (ordinality);
- order a group of familiar numbers;
- read familiar larger numbers – the number of children in the class, door numbers, bus numbers and so on;
- use words such as 'more than', 'less than' and 'the same as' when comparing numbers to 10;
- give a number that comes between two others (eg suggest a number that can be found on the number line between 5 and 9).

YEAR 1/PRIMARY 2

Counting:
- accurately count a set of at least 20 objects;
- count forwards or backwards in 1s from any number to at least 100 and back to at least 0;
- count on or back in 10s from any multiple of 10 (100, 90, 80, ... 0 or 50, 60, 70, ...);
- count in 2s, knowing which set of numbers is odd and which is even;
- know that numbers can indicate quantity of position in a line or series.

Reading and ordering:
- read numerals and words to at least 50;
- order a set of sequential numbers to at least 50 (for example 34, 36, 33, 35 and 32);
- understand and explain that 17 is 10 + 7;
- know the equivalence between ten 1p coins and one 10p coin;
- show that 17p can be represented by a 10p coin and 7 × 1p coins or model 17 with Base 10 apparatus;
- recognise a half ($\frac{1}{2}$) and a quarter ($\frac{1}{4}$).

YEAR 2/PRIMARY 3

Counting:
- count a set of up to 100 objects, grouping in 10s to facilitate the count;
- count on or back in 1s, 10s or 100s from any number;
- count in 2s, 3s, 4s or 5s from a small number to at least 30;
- count back in 5s beyond 0 from any multiple of 5 (95, 90, 85, 80 ... –10, –15).

Reading and ordering:
- numerals and words to at least 1000 (one thousand);
- know that 53 is 50 + 3 and be able to make 53p with 10p and 1p coins or model with Base 10 apparatus;
- order any two- or three-digit numbers (such as 123, 90, 23, 9 and 132);
- be familiar with 'decimals' in the context of money;
- understand the equivalence of the coins;
- recognise a half ($\frac{1}{2}$), a quarter ($\frac{1}{4}$) and a third ($\frac{1}{3}$) of a whole and of a quantity (for example, shade a half of a circle or indicate one third of a collection of counters);
- understand the equivalence of a half and two quarters.

Children need to be given many different opportunities to count. Confidence in counting, and subsequent familiarity with the number system, is necessary if children are to acquire further number skills, and can only be achieved by the children having many diverse opportunities to practise on a regular basis. It will help if the children can hear, see and touch objects and numbers. This will assist them in making their own mental images.

Resources such as number lines and 100 squares should be permanently displayed in the classroom so that the number system can become a familiar part of their everyday classroom life. It is important to refer children's attention to these and make as much use of them as possible.

Every classroom should have a long number line; up to at least 100 for Year 2 children. Different colours or shapes for alternate 10s will help children to use the line and see its structure. Number lines can be extended into negative numbers at this stage too.
A number line is useful for:

seeing the number order;
recognising numbers;
identifying the numbers that come before, after and between each number;
number patterns;
seeing the significance of place value by recognising a new colour and noticing that the 10s number has changed.

Similarly, familiarity with a 100 square can reinforce patterns in the number system. The 0–99 square is useful because each new decade starts a new row:

0	1	2	3	4	5	6	7	8	9
10	11	12	13	14	15	16	17	18	19
20	21	22	23	24	25				
30	31								

Children should be encouraged to count on numbers over 10 by moving down and along rather than counting in ones and moving solely along the lines.

23 + 15 → count down one row for 10 and along five squares for the 5:

	...	22	**23**	24	25	26	27	28	29
30	31	32	**33**	**34**	**35**	**36**	**37**	**38**	39

Number names When children count, listen very carefully to their pronunciation of the 'teen' and 'ty' numbers. Sometimes young children will count in 10s and say '10, 20, 13, 14, 15, 16, 17, 18, 19'. This can lead them into thinking that the next number is 20 (rather than 100). It is unfortunate that the teen numbers do not follow the same pattern as the rest of the number system. In the 'teens' it is the second part of the name that indicates the value of the tens, in the rest of the number system we read as we write with the tens value coming first:

17 *seven*teen (rather than *onety-seven!*)
71 *seventy-one*

This is a common source of confusion for a lot of children. For this reason it is important not to restrict children to numbers less than 20 which will hinder their understanding; better to discuss the fact that the 'teen' numbers are named differently and so care must be taken. Correct any mispronunciation immediately, encouraging children to listen carefully to the sounds of the two words.

Reading numbers correctly requires an understanding of the place value involved. Discourage children from reading larger numbers digit by digit as in a telephone number:

'seven hundred and three' NOT 'seven-oh(!)-three'

DEVELOPING MENTAL MATHS

COUNTING AND ORDERING *(vertical, left margin)*

COUNTING TO 5

†† *Whole class sitting in a semicircle with the teacher sitting in the space*
⏲ *About 10 minutes*

AIMS
To count and recognise numbers up to 5. To know the order of numbers.

YOU WILL NEED
A large piece of paper, a thick felt-tipped pen.

WHAT TO DO
This activity concentrates on counting and recognising the numbers up to 5, but you may need to begin with the numbers 1–3 and extend to 5, and later up to 10.

Go around the circle and ask each child to take a turn counting one number up to five. When you reach your first five, ask these children to come into the centre of the semicircle and sit in a line in order.

Let the children continue counting up to 5 and making rows until all the children have been placed. You may have one short row.

Now ask all the children who are number 1 to stand up. Ask the class, 'How many claps for 1?' Encourage the number 1 children to clap once. Repeat with the other numbers, checking that the children are counting in unison by counting and clapping together.

DISCUSSION QUESTIONS
Write a number (either between 1–3 or 1–5 depending on which numbers you have used on the paper and show it to the children:
● *Can you put up your hand if you are this number?*
● *What is the number?*
If possible extend this by asking:
● *Can you stand up if you are one more than this number?*
● *Can those children standing up clap and count their number?*

ASSESSMENT QUESTIONS
● *By observing the children it will be apparent which children are finding the task difficult. It may be helpful to place these children near the beginning of the count.*
● *Ask a child to come to the front and name all the children who are 'number 3'.*

WHERE SHALL WE PUT THE NUMBER?

†† *Ten children sitting in a wide semicircle*
⏲ *About 10 minutes*

AIM
To develop a mental image of a number line.

YOU WILL NEED
A skipping rope, a set of large number cards (1–5 to begin with, but extend to 20 later).

WHAT TO DO
Shuffle the number cards and place them face down in the space in front of the children. Lay the skipping rope in a straight line in the gap. Ask the children to imagine that the rope is a number line which begins on their left with 1 and ends on their right with 5 (or 10 or 20 depending on how far you have extended the numbers).

Ask a child to pick up a number card, and tell you what the number is called (for example, 6). He or she can then choose where on the 'number line' to place the number. Do all the children agree with the position? Continue asking the children to pick and place the cards.

DISCUSSION QUESTIONS
● *Can you explain why 6 is in the right place?*
● *Does this number (7) come before or after 6?*
● *How many numbers will we need to fill this space? (Indicate the space between 7 and the end of the rope.)*

ASSESSMENT

Note whether the children are able to explain their decisions. Can they explain why 5 will be near the middle and 9 further towards the end?

EXTENSIONS

When all the cards are arranged in the correct order, ask the children to turn around while you rearrange part of the number line. For example:
● turn one card over;
● interchange the positions of two of the cards;
● turn a card upside down.
 Tell the children to turn round and ask them:
● Can you explain what has happened?
● How can you put it right?
 Use sequences of cards that do not start at 1, for example 4–12 or 3–33, or count in 2s or 3s from 0 or a multiple of the count number, for example 6. Try making the line a decreasing number line, for instance starting from 20 on the right.

KEEP FIT MATHS

†† *Whole class sitting in a semicircle with the teacher sitting in the space*
🕐 *About 5 minutes*

AIM

To introduce the children to using their fingers as a counting aid.

WHAT TO DO

Some children need to be 'given permission' to use their fingers to count. They need to recognise one hand as being worth 5 without counting each finger every time. The children will then be able to use their fingers to count, first up to 5 and then up to 10 on future occasions. Ask the children to hold up one folded hand and to touch and raise one finger at a time as they count up to 5.

DISCUSSION QUESTIONS

● *Who can quickly show me five fingers without counting?*
● *How can we check that we are right?*
Encourage the children to check by folding their fingers down as they count.

ASSESSMENT QUESTIONS

Ask how many fingers are folded down. Say:
● *Show me four fingers. How many are folded down? (1)*
● *How do you know? (Because 4 and 1 makes 5.)*
 With this particular example, the youngest children often feel very pleased with themselves because they can see the knuckle of the folded

thumb as the missing 1, and so have a strategy for getting the answer!

EXTENSION

When the children can count and show fingers to represent numbers up to 5, extend the activity up to 10 by using both hands.

KEEPING VERY FIT

†† *Whole class sitting in a semicircle with their legs folded or tucked underneath them with the teacher in the gap*
🕐 *A few minutes two or three times a week until the children are confident*

AIM

To offer a strategy for counting up to 20 in 5s and 1s using hands and feet.

WHAT TO DO

In this activity the children use their hands and feet to count up to 20 in 5s and 1s. Their feet, with ten toes, represent 10.
 Show the children how they can count to 5 and 10 by putting their legs out in front of them (be careful that nobody gets kicked). Explain that they can count on up to 20 by raising one finger at a time and counting in unison: 11,12... .
 Once the children are confident with this begin counting back. Begin the count by 'putting 20 in

COUNTING AND ORDERING

your head'. Gently place both hands on your head and say 20. Now count back by folding down one digit at a time and saying 19, 18… . At 10 fold one leg away and say 5. Then fold the other leg and say 0 (nought).

ASSESSMENT
Check that children are saying the teen numbers properly, that is '13' and not '30', and that the counting matches the hand movements.

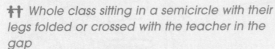

IN THEIR TEENS

†† *Whole class sitting in a semicircle with their legs folded or crossed with the teacher in the gap*
🕐 *A few minutes several times a week*

AIMS
To match objects to a number by counting on or counting back. To emphasise the order and pattern of the teen numbers in order to begin developing understanding of place value.

YOU WILL NEED
Two 10p coins and nine 1p coins (or two ten-sticks of cubes and nine units).

WHAT TO DO
You will want the children to know that:
● 14 take away 4 is 10;
● 14 take away 10 is 4;
● 10 add on 4 is 14;
● 4 add on 10 is 14;
and so on for all the teen numbers from 10 + 1 to 10 + 10. These need to be practised so that the children can begin to make mental images.

Lay out the coins, left to right, for example one 10p and four 1p coins.

Ask the children 'Can you show me with your hands and feet the amount of money on the carpet?' The children should stretch out their legs to show 10 and hold up the correct number of fingers.

DISCUSSION QUESTIONS
● *How do you know that what you are showing is the same as the money?*
● *Show me what it will be if I take away 10?*
(The children should fold or cross their legs – check by removing the 10p.)

Replace the 10p:
● *What is it now?*
● *What if I take away three pennies?*
Continue playing until the children are quick and confident with all the pairs from 10 to 20.

EXTENSION
You will need a set of 0–20 number cards. Choose cards at random and ask the children to represent them with their hands and feet.

FILLING TIME

†† *Whole class* 🕐 *Any odd moments*

AIM
To model numbers in various ways, initially to 10.

WHAT TO DO
Many of the following ideas can be practised during odd moments, such as waiting for the end of a session, at hometime or after taking the register. Ask the children any of the following types of questions, referring where appropriate to familiar classroom resources:
● Can you show me four fingers?
● Can we clap and count 6 for Sam's birthday? (It is important that the children count and clap in unison.)
● Hassan, please can you show us how we can find out how many pencils your group needs today?
● Who can count along the number line and stop at number 8? (Check that the child touches each number as it is spoken.)
● Who can find number 7 on the number line?

● Can you count on to number 11?
● Who can point to the number for these jumps? (Secretly ask a child to jump a number of times for you.)

Singing and acting out number songs and chants is a common part of early years' practice and is a useful way of reinforcing number names and sequence without an overt 'maths' focus.

DISCUSSION QUESTIONS

Follow up each activity of this type with questions which require the children to explain how they got to the answer. For example:

● *Mary, how were you able to show six fingers without counting?*

Mary might reply: 'Five fingers on this hand, add on one more is six.'

● *Sarah, how did you know which number to point to on the number line?*

Sarah might 'just know' what 7, for example, looks like, or she may know that it comes after 5 and before 10, or she may have counted along the number line carefully until she got there.

Unless very convoluted, model each method for the other children so they are clear how it worked.

THE METRE RULER

†† *Whole class facing the teacher*
🕐 *About 5 minutes*

AIMS

To count in 10s up to 100. To model the size of a number in relation to its place value. To introduce approximation.

YOU WILL NEED

A metre ruler demarcated into decimetres and coloured in with two alternating colours (no numbers).

WHAT TO DO

Using the ruler as a model number line, practise counting in 10s from 0 up to 100 and back down by pointing to each decimetre. Try beginning at other numbers which are multiples of 10 and counting forwards or back. Then point to individual decimetres and question the children about their position.

DISCUSSION QUESTIONS

● *Is this number nearer 0 or nearer 100?*
● *Is this number bigger or smaller than 50?*
● *What is the number?*
● *How do you know?*
● *Did anyone use a different method?*

EXTENSION

When the children are confident with the tens, begin using the numbers between the decimetres. Ask the children to consider similar questions. Point to a position, for example 42:

● Is this number nearer 40 or 50?
● Does the number come somewhere near the middle?
● Who can come out and point to a number between 30 and 40, that is closer to 30 than 40? What numbers could you point to?

CONKERS

†† *Whole class sitting in a semicircle with the teacher in the space*
🕐 *About 10 minutes*

AIMS

To find a strategy for counting large numbers of objects. To demonstrate how being systematic aids checking.

YOU WILL NEED

A large number of objects, for example a big bag of conkers.

WHAT TO DO

Empty the conkers on to the floor and ask the children a question such as 'How can we find out how many conkers Jon has brought to school?'

It is often best to model the beginning of the count. Say something such as, 'I am going to count the conkers in groups of 10'. Count out two groups of 10 and ask how many conkers you have counted. Why do the children think you are counting in 10s? Ask some children to come out and continue counting the conkers into further groups of 10.

COUNTING AND ORDERING

DISCUSSION QUESTIONS
● *How many groups of ten conkers are there altogether?*
● *Who can count them in 10s?*
● *How many 1s are left over?*
● *How is the number written?*

EXTENSION
Provide a large box of multicoloured cubes. Organise the children into pairs and ask each pair to choose a colour to sort and count. Tell the children you would like the cubes to be sorted into groups so that you can check their count.

Encourage them to estimate first by writing down how many cubes they think there are. When they have sorted the cubes, discuss their ideas and then let them decide how to record their work. The children will need to write down their totals, perhaps using a number line to help. When they have finished, ask the pairs of children to sit in a circle around their cubes and report back their findings. Write these on a large sheet of paper, for example the colour which had the smallest number. Together rewrite the colours and numbers in order. Give groups large collections to organise and count for themselves. Discuss whether 10s was the most useful grouping – did they try 2s or 5s instead?

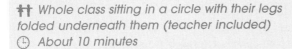

COUNTING IN 2S

†† *Whole class sitting in a circle with their legs folded underneath them (teacher included)*
⏱ *About 10 minutes*

AIM
To count on and back in 2s with even numbers.

WHAT TO DO
Discuss with the children the number of legs in the room. They may suggest that it is double the number of people present. Write down their suggestions and make suitable comments.

Ask the children to unfold their legs as they count and to count round the circle 1, **2**, 3, **4** and so on. They should whisper the odd number and speak the even number. It is surprising how quickly the children will be able to count in 2s.

DISCUSSION QUESTIONS
● *How many legs are there in this circle?*
● *Will there be more or fewer legs than people?*
● *How do you know? How can we find out?*
● *How many legs have ten people got? (Draw attention to the fact that there are twice as many legs as people and half as many people as legs.)*

VARIATIONS
● Will the answer be smaller, larger or the same if we count our arms?
● How do you know?
● How can we find out?

EXTENSION
● Count back in 2s by asking the children to say the numbers and fold their legs.

THROWING NUMBERS

†† *Whole class sitting facing the teacher*
⏱ *About 5 minutes*

AIM
To begin to recognise the significance of place value.

YOU WILL NEED
A large sheet of paper pinned up where the children can all see it, a felt-tipped pen.

WHAT TO DO
Write a number on the sheet, for example 10. Make sure that the children can read the number and know how many 10s it contains. Then explain you are going to 'throw out this number'. Demonstrate by holding out both hands, shooting out your fingers and saying 'Ten'.

Try with other multiples of ten, for example 30. Throw out your hands three times and say '10, 20, 30'. When the children have done this several times and seem confident, use the other numbers. For example, 27 is two hand throws and a 7 (saying 10, 20, 25, 26, 27). It is important to throw out your hands and count in unison.

DISCUSSION QUESTIONS
● *Who can show me what 10 more/less than this number would be? How do you know?*
● *Can you write that number?*
● *What do you notice about the numbers?*

VARIATION
Ask a child to come out and 'throw' a number. Then choose another child to write the number on the board and 'throw out' another number. Continue until every child has had a turn.

EXTENSION
Ask the children to write extended number sentences that represent what they have done, for instance, 30 + 7 = 37.

MAKING A NUMBER LINE

†† *About ten children sitting in a line*
🕐 *About 15 minutes*

AIM
To order numbers using place value.

YOU WILL NEED
A set of number cards from 0–50, an area long enough in which to place this number line.

WHAT TO DO
Give each child about five cards to arrange in order in front of him or her. Tell the children that together you are going to make a number line. Ask:
● On which side shall we begin our number line?
● Who has the number to begin our line?
   Explain that they will need to watch carefully so that they know when to come out and place their cards in the line.

DISCUSSION QUESTIONS
● *Who has the next number?*
● *How do you know you are next?*

VARIATION
Lay out the cards as above (in a number line) and ask each child to pick a coloured cube. Then choose a rule for the day, such as 'Count on 2'; 'Count on 5'; 'Count back 5', and so on. Ask the first child to place his or her cube on 0. The second child follows the rule for that day, for instance 'Count on 2' and places his or her cube on the correct number. Continue until all the children have had a turn. Then ask:
● Can you see a pattern?
● Who can explain the pattern?

● Shall we read the numbers with cubes together?
● Can you read the numbers without cubes?
● Can you read the numbers with cubes beginning with 20?

EXTENSION
When the children are confident with this, move on to make and explore a 0–100 line. Try ordering sets of numbers that do not start at 0, for example 7–35, or sets of non-sequential numbers.

ROWS OF TEN

†† *Whole class sitting in a large circle*
🕐 *About 5 minutes*

AIM
To develop place value, and highlight the value of counting with 10s and 1s.

WHAT TO DO
Ask the children to count round the circle up to 10. Ask these children to make a row of ten in the centre of the circle. Continue counting and arranging the children in rows of ten. You may have one short row. Ask the children how many rows of ten there are and how many are left over. This will help to introduce the idea of place value. For example, three rows of ten children makes 30, and two more children makes 32.
   Encourage the children to listen to the pattern as the numbers are said. Point out that each row begins with a one (11, 21, 31...). If the children have not noticed this write these numbers on the board or refer the children to the number line. Say to them, 'Stand up if your number has two 1s in it (for instance 2, 12, 22, 32...). Can you say your numbers to the rest of the class?'

COUNTING AND ORDERING

DISCUSSION QUESTIONS
● *What do you notice about all the numbers which have two 1s?*
● *Can someone come out and tell us all the children whose numbers have five 1s (for example 5, 15, 25...)?*
● *If Hanif is number 3, who is 10 more than him? Where is he or she sitting?*
● *Patrick is number 29. Who is 10 less than that? Where is she or he sitting? What do you notice?*

EXTENSION
Use a 0–99 square and locate numbers 10 more/ 10 less than the starting numbers.

MAKING A 0–49 NUMBER RECTANGLE

†† *Ten children working in pairs on the floor*
🕐 *About 15 minutes*

AIM
To develop place value, and emphasise the pattern of numbers up to 49.

YOU WILL NEED
A set of 0–49 number cards.

WHAT TO DO
Pair a more able child with a less confident child, or a younger child with an older one and give these pairs their cards at the beginning of the count. Give each pair ten cards, for example 0–9, or 10–19 or 20–29 and so on, and ask them to arrange their cards in order.

Encourage each pair to point at and read their smallest number. When they have done this, ask them to arrange their cards in a pile so that the smallest number is at the top and the biggest number is at the bottom. Bring the children together and ask them to lay out each pile of cards in a row, one below the other, to form a number rectangle.

DISCUSSION QUESTIONS
Ask each pair to look at their pile of ordered cards:
● *Who has the cards without any tens?*
● *Can you arrange the cards in lines?*
● *Who has the set of cards to put in a line under the no tens line?*
● *How do you know?*
Continue questioning like this while building the rectangle until all the cards have been positioned. What strategies do the children have, and which information do they use, to place the cards?
Then discuss the complete rectangle:
● *Can you see any patterns in the rectangle?*
● *What patterns can you see?*

ASSESSMENT
Can the children:
● read the numbers?
● find a number by using the pattern?
● arrange the numbers in order?
● see that each row has the same tens number?
● see that each column has the same units number?
● see that each row begins with a multiple of ten?

VARIATIONS
● Ask one child to turn round while another child removes a card. Tell the first child to turn back and ask him or her which card has been taken. Continue until every child has had a turn at both removing a card and guessing the missing number. Each time, ask the child how he or she knew which number was missing.
● Ask questions about the rectangle such as 'I am thinking of a number which comes between 37 and 39. Who can say which number I am thinking about?' or 'I am thinking of a number that is 4 more than 12. Who can explain which number it is?'

EXTENSIONS
● Once the children are comfortable with this increase the number cards to 99.
● Use an almost blank 10 × 10 grid, and ask the children where particular numbers will go.

0				5					
	21								

Where would 7, 27 and 87 go?

MAKING NUMBERS

†† *About 15 children arranged in a long line*
🕐 *About 10 minutes*

AIM
To emphasise the significance of place value by repositioning numbers.

YOU WILL NEED
Three sets of 0–9 number cards (enough for each child to have two cards).

WHAT TO DO
Shuffle the cards and deal out two to each child. Ask the children to arrange their card so as to make the smallest number possible. For instance if the child has the number cards 2 and 1 the lowest number would be 12.

Ask the children to place their cards down on the floor. Let the children take turns to read out their numbers. Then ask the child with the smallest number to put up his or her hand. Check that everyone agrees, then ask that child to move to sit at the start of the row. Then find who has the next smallest number. Ask this child to move to sit next to the first child. Continue until all the children are in order, then ask them to take turns to read out their numbers to check that the order is correct.

Next ask the children to arrange their cards so as to make the biggest number possible and read them out. They will find they are now out of order, so allow the children to move about and try to reorder themselves. They can check the order by counting in turn and holding up their number cards as each number is called out.

DISCUSSION QUESTIONS
Once everyone has made a new number:
● *Has any one made the same number?*
● *Are we still sitting in the correct order?*
● *How quickly can you get into the correct order?*
● *How can we check that we are right?*

EXTENSIONS
● Give the children three digit cards each. How many numbers can they make with them? In how many different ways can they reorder themselves, depending which numbers they have made? Start with everyone's largest/smallest number.
● Give each child initially two, and later three, digit cards, but include lots of 0s for example 100–110 and 200–210. Emphasise, for example, that 'one hundred and seven' is 1–0–7, and not 100–7, as it sounds when spoken.

ONE MORE, ONE LESS

†† *Whole class sitting in a semicircle with the teacher sitting in the space*
🕐 *About 5 minutes*

AIM
To recognise and model one more and one less.

WHAT TO DO
Ask the children a question such as 'Who can quickly show me 4? Who can show me one more than 4?'

Look for the children modelling the question with their hands. Another child may point to or describe the number line and move along it. You or the children may also like to incorporate a story to reflect the numbers you have used. 'I have four sweets. My friend gives me one more – now I have five'.

DISCUSSION
For each number, and for numbers 1 more or less than that, ask various children to explain how they found the answer.

ASSESSMENT
See if the children can model the inverse, in this case, 4 as 'one less' than 5. For example, hold up one hand and say, 'This hand shows 5, fold down one finger and I have 4.' Encourage all the children to copy this: 'Five fingers, fold down one and we have four.'

You may like to record this example on the chalkboard. This will help the children make the connection between the practical example and the visual algorithm.

BEFORE AND AFTER

†† Whole class sitting in a semicircle
⏲ 15 minutes

AIMS
To recognise the numbers which come before and after all numbers up to 100. To extend one more/one less.

YOU WILL NEED
A large sheet of paper pinned up for all the children to see, a thick felt-tipped pen, paper, pencils.

WHAT TO DO
Write a number, for example 46, at the top of your sheet, leaving room either side.

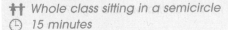

Show it to the class and ask the children, 'Who can read this number? Who can write the number that is 1 bigger to the right of 46? Can you read the new number? Can you write the number that is 1 less on the left-hand side? Who can read that number? Can you write the number that is 10 bigger than 46 in the middle of your paper? Write the numbers that are 1 bigger and 1 smaller on either side of 56. Can you read your numbers so that I can write them on my sheet?'

Ask the children to read out their numbers and write them on to your sheet. Try other numbers.

DISCUSSION QUESTIONS
● *How did you choose the number 10 bigger than mine?*
● *What do you notice about the numbers?*
● *Can you carry on the pattern?*
● *How do you know what to write next?*

EXTENSIONS
● Use other numbers and ask the children to make them 2 more and 2 less. Note that this activity becomes difficult for children when they need to go over into new multiples of ten (bridging a decade).
● This activity can be used for small groups working with 0–9 number cards. Each child makes a two-digit number. Tasks can then be set to reflect the abilities of the groups, for example, 'Make the number 2 bigger and 2 smaller.'

COUNT ON

†† Whole class facing the teacher
⏲ About 5 minutes twice a week

AIMS
To count on from any number less than 20 (with fingers). To write the numbers 1–20. To begin to use number symbols to represent a problem.

YOU WILL NEED
A large sheet of paper, a thick felt-tipped pen.

WHAT TO DO
Write a number on the sheet of paper, for example 12. Ask the children if they can read the number. Do they know what the answer will be if you count on 4? Model this by 'putting 12 in your head' (put your hands on your head to put in the 12) and counting on 4. Hold up four fingers and fold each finger down as you count.

DISCUSSION QUESTIONS
● *Who can come up and write the number we have ended on?*
As the children become more confident, especially with recording, ask:
● *Who can come and write a number sentence to show what we have just done?*

ASSESSMENT QUESTION
Who can count to show us what this number sentence means: 18 – 3 = 15? (Put 18 in your head, hold up three fingers and say '17, 16, 15' as you fold away each finger.)

EXTENSIONS
● When the children are confident counting on and back in 1s from numbers less than 20, try counting in 2s, 5s or 10s.
● Extend to starting with any two-digit number and counting on and back in 2s, 5s or 10s. Ask questions such as 'If we start at 12 and count in 2s what numbers will we say? Who can count back in 2s from 18? If I start at 10 and count on five 2s, what number will I end up at?'

LUNCHTIME

†† *Up to four children working in pairs to solve the problem*
⏱ *About 10 minutes*

AIMS

To practise counting and matching one-to-one. To devise a method for solving a counting problem in the context of setting and laying a table successfully.

YOU WILL NEED

A table, several chairs, toys to occupy the chairs, cutlery and a tea set. Paper and pencils for recording.

WHAT TO DO

Ask the children to set the table for the toys' tea party. Encourage them to think of a way of recording their work.

DISCUSSION QUESTIONS

● *Can you explain how you knew how many plates to use?*
● *Can you explain how you have recorded your work?*
● *How will we know, from your work, how many plates you needed?*
● *Could we show this in any other way?*
● *How many plates would you need if three more friends came to tea?*

ASSESSMENT

Consider how the children solved the problem. Did they count first? Were they using this information to make other decisions? How was the information recorded?

VARIATIONS

● Ask the children to solve the problem without apparatus so that they cannot physically see how many items they have laid out.
● Set verbal problems such as 'Ten children are going on a picnic. Each child will need three sandwiches, a drink and two cakes. How much food will you need to take for everyone?'

REGISTER MATHS

†† *Whole class sitting in a large circle*
⏱ *A few minutes each day*

AIMS

To count on and count back up to 30 (or more). To know that the last number in the count represents the size of the count.

WHAT TO DO

This is an excellent activity to begin the day. It reinforces the idea that the last number of a count is the number of objects counted. The activity can be extended and adapted very quickly and easily. It encourages good concentration and supportive attitudes.

Ask the children how they can find out how many pupils are in the class today. The children will say by counting. Ask 'Shall we count ourselves?'

Select one child to begin the count. The children then take turns to say a number 1, 2, 3 and so on until everyone in the class has had a turn.

Ask a child to find the number on the class number line. It is essential that children understand that the total number will stay the same unless some things are added or taken away.

DISCUSSION QUESTIONS

● *Will the answer be the same if we begin with someone else? How do you know?*
● *Shall we try again beginning with Amy? Was the number the same? Why?*
● *Why is today's number different from yesterday's?*

VARIATIONS

● Ask questions such as 'How many heads, noses, mouths are there in the circle? How do you know?'
● Join the circle yourself and ask, 'How many are in the circle now? How do you know?'

EXTENSIONS

● Stand up if your number is bigger than 10.
● Stand up if your number is smaller than 18.
● Stand up if your number is bigger than 12 but smaller than 22 and so on.

DOGGY FRACTIONS

†† *About 10 children working in pairs*
🕐 *About 15 minutes*

AIM

To develop strategies for solving problems using fractions.

YOU WILL NEED

A copy of photocopiable page 63 for each pair, pencils and colouring materials, a series of questions for the children appropriate to their ability written on the chalkboard.

WHAT TO DO

Organise the children into pairs and ask each pair to look closely at photocopiable page 63. Explain that they will need to listen carefully, and follow your instructions where necessary, in order to answer your questions.

● Half the dogs ran out of the park after a cat, how many dogs stayed in the park?
● Four dogs played with a ball, what fraction of all the dogs is that?
● Colour half the dogs black.
● Colour half of the remainder brown.
● How many white dogs are there? What fraction of all the dogs is that?
● How many dogs have you coloured? What fraction of all the dogs is that?

DISCUSSION QUESTIONS

● *How many is 'half' the dogs?*
● *How did you find that out?*

ASSESSMENT

Look for the children's strategies for calculating the fractions. Do they understand that half of 12 is 6, and colour six dogs? Do they begin colouring and then try to solve the problem?

EXTENSIONS

● Give each child some blank paper and ask each pair to draw a different number of objects or animals. Then ask similar questions.
● Ask each pair to make a Multilink snake using two colours, half in one colour and half in another. Do the children know that they will need an even number of cubes? Do they count out a certain number of one colour then double this number with another colour? Or do they use the sharing method (1 red, 1 green; 1 red, 1 green)? Each method should be demonstrated and discussed.
● Discuss 'half size' by cutting out a paper snake that is 16cm long. Cut out another snake half its length and ask the children how long this snake is. Do they know how many snakes would be needed to fit along the first snake? How do they know? What fraction of the big snake will the smaller snakes be? Ask the children if they can cut out a snake a quarter of the size of the first snake.

HOW OLD ARE WE?

†† *Whole class, then groups of about 10 children building up the information*
🕐 *About 10 minutes for the initial activity*

AIMS

To enable the children to sort themselves using two categories. To extract information from a Carroll diagram.

YOU WILL NEED

A large prepared sheet of paper (see illustration below), a small piece of paper for each child, adhesive, pencils, a series of questions for the children appropriate to their ability written on the chalkboard.

WHAT TO DO

Hand each child a small piece of paper and ask them to draw their faces and then to write their name beside their picture.

Attach the large sheet of paper to the wall and read the categories together. Tell the children that

	boys	girls
6 years old		
7 years old		

they are each going to stick their picture in one of the sections. Point to one section, for example 6-year-old boys, and ask the children to put their hands up if they think their pictures are appropriate for this section. How do they know?

22

HOW TALL ARE WE?

†† *About 10 children working in pairs*
🕐 *About 20 minutes*

AIMS

To gather and order numerical information, using hundreds numbers. To find differences.

YOU WILL NEED

Metre sticks, felt-tipped pens, Blu-Tack, individual sheets of paper, a large sheet to record the group information, list of questions written on the board.

WHAT TO DO

Ask the children to work in pairs to measure their heights. They should record this information collectively on the large sheet of paper. When they have all done this, ask the pairs of children to write the information in order on their own sheets of paper and then count or calculate to find out the answers to the questions on the board:

● How many children are taller (shorter) than you?
● How much taller is the tallest person than you?
● How many children are shorter than 120cm?
● Are there any children that have a difference in height of exactly 10cm?

Discuss the children's strategies for finding the differences between their heights. They may suggest: 'We counted on using the metre sticks – 114, 124, 125, 126, 127, 128... 14cm'; 'I counted back from Mark's height of 128cm to 117cm, 128, 118, 117... 11cm.' It may be helpful to encourage the children to use Blu-Tack to mark the two numbers in order to count between them.

DISCUSSION QUESTIONS

● *Are you sure this number should go before that one? Jenny looks taller than Kelly, but should her height be bigger or smaller? Do we need to check our measuring?*
● *Naayab, can you explain how you found the difference between your height and Bethan's?*

VARIATIONS

● Tell the children to make Plasticine snakes 20cm long. How many grams will balance your snake?
● Use the class calendar to find how many days between significant dates. How many days between Joe's birthday and Imogen's birthday? How many more days before the holidays?

EXTENSION

'If I laid the whole class end to end how far would you stretch? Would that be longer or shorter than the playground?'

Choose about ten children to begin with (it may be best to choose younger children, the others can keep their pictures for later when they can place their drawings independently) and ask them to place their pictures in the category they think is correct. When they have done this, refer them to the questions you have written on the board. Ask:

● How many 6-year-old boys/girls?
● How many 7-year-old boys/girls?
● How many boys/girls?
● Can you explain why you have put your picture there?
● Which section has the largest number of children?

Repeat this process until all the children have contributed to the chart, counting and comparing the numbers of children in each section of the chart each time.

DISCUSSION QUESTIONS

● *Sam, where is your picture going to fit? Will it fit in here (for example, pointing to '7-year-old boys')? Why/why not? (He's 6½)*
● *When will you be able to put it in that section? (After his next birthday.)*
● *Which sections will it never go into? Why? (The 'girls' section.)*
● *Will the number of boys stay the same? Will the number of 6-year-old boys stay the same? Can you explain your reasons?*

VARIATIONS

Choose different categories for the Carroll diagram, for instance: Walk to school/don't walk to school/boys/girls; Wearing lace-ups today/not wearing lace-ups today; have a spring or summer birthday/have an autumn or winter birthday.

COUNTING AND ORDERING

ON 10 MORE

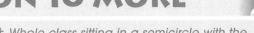

†† *Whole class sitting in a semicircle with the teacher in the space*
⊕ *10 minutes*

AIM
To count on and back in 10s from any number.

YOU WILL NEED
Nine ten-sticks and nine unit cubes (or nine 10p coins and nine 1p coins), a large sheet of paper, a felt-tipped pen, a copy of photocopiable page 64 for each child (optional).

WHAT TO DO
Lay out three 10s and five 1s (cubes or coins) and ask the children to count the apparatus in their minds. Then choose one child to write the number on the sheet of paper. Next ask what the number will be if one more ten is placed on the floor. Choose another child to write the new number.

Keep adding 10s, each time asking the children to write the numbers on the sheet in order to demonstrate the written and visual pattern of adding a ten.

Follow-up this activity by using the writing frame on photocopiable page 64.

DISCUSSION QUESTIONS
After a ten has been added and the new number written up, ask:
● *Do we agree?*
● *Who can explain why the answer is right?*
● *Which number changed?*
● *Why has the units number stayed the same?*

EXTENSIONS
● Try taking away 10s and asking the children what these numbers are.
● Ask more complex questions such as 'Who can write the answer if I take away 21? Who can change the apparatus to show the answer?'

Encourage the children to describe what they are doing.
● Continue into three-digit numbers with Base 10 'flats, longs and small cubes'. Lay out three flats, two longs and four unit cubes. Choose one child to write the number on the large sheet of paper. Ask the children to read the number. They may need encouragement to read the number correctly, that is three hundred and twenty four and not three two four.

KEEPING A SECRET

†† *About ten children*
⊕ *About 10 minutes*

AIM
To recognise the position of a number from its place value.

YOU WILL NEED
A set of 0–9 number cards, a large sheet of paper, a thick felt-tipped pen, a copy of photocopiable page 64 for each child (optional).

WHAT TO DO
You may need to model this activity before asking the children to try it. Shuffle the number cards and ask one child to come out, pick two cards and secretly make a number with them. Ask the child to give the class a clue to help them guess the number (for instance, 'My number is one more than 25').

Once they have guessed ask the child to show his or her cards to the class. Ask the children: 'Who can write the number on the large sheet of paper?' Does the written number match the card number?

When the children seem confident with the exercise, more difficult clues can be given such as 'It is 10 more/less than 15'. They could follow-up this activity by using the writing frame on photocopiable page 64.

DISCUSSION QUESTIONS
● *Which clues are easiest to use? Why?*
● *Which numbers are hardest to guess? Why?*
● *What other clues could we give for this number?*

EXTENSION
The children can make a class flap book of number clues for display in the classroom.

GUESS THE NUMBER

†† *Whole class facing the teacher*
🕐 *About 5 minutes*

AIM
To develop visualisation skills by recognising the position of numbers on an imaginary line.

YOU WILL NEED
A metre ruler that has one plain side, Blu-Tack, paper, pencils, a copy of photocopiable page 64 for each child (optional).

WHAT TO DO
Hold the ruler with the numbered side towards you and upside down. Place a small piece of Blu-Tack on the blank side/lower edge of the metre ruler. Ask the children to write down the number on

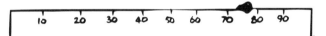

which they think the Blu-Tack has been placed. Invite several children to read out the number they have written. Roll the ruler over to see who was closest. The numbers will now be the right way up.

It is almost impossible to be exactly right, so give praise for close approximations.

Can the children describe their thoughts and the maths here using photocopiable page 64?

DISCUSSION QUESTIONS
● *Can you explain why you have written that number?*
● *Which numbers are most difficult to estimate their positions? Which numbers are easiest? Why?*

NEGATIVE NUMBERS

†† *About 15 children*
🕐 *About 10 minutes for each part. Allow 30 minutes for the temperature reading to fall*

AIM
To explore the significance of negative numbers.

YOU WILL NEED
A large spirit thermometer (that can measure below 0°C), chalkboard, access to a refrigerator, a bag of ice, pencil and a copy of photocopiable page 64 for each child (optional).

WHAT TO DO
Hold up the thermometer and ask the children if they know what it is used for. Do they know what the numbers down the side are for? Do they know what would happen to the liquid inside the thermometer if it was placed over the radiator? Try it to find out. Ask if anyone can explain what has happened? Record the children's ideas, and any changes observed, on the chalkboard.

What do the children think will happen if the thermometer is placed against a shady wall? Do this. Can the children explain why this happens?

Finally ask if they know anywhere colder you can put the thermometer. What do they think will happen? Put the thermometer in the refrigerator or, better still, the freezer compartment and leave it for approximately 30 minutes. What number is the liquid level at now? Do any of the children know how to read the numbers below zero? Explain how to do this and read the numbers together. Keep the thermometer in a bag of ice while you talk about it in order to keep the thermometer at a low temperature (at least 0°C).

The children can record and reflect on this investigation by using photocopiable page 64.

DISCUSSION QUESTIONS
● *What happens when you count back – do you have to stop at 0? Can you remember how to read the numbers below zero? Shall we write these in the squares?*
Before taking the thermometer out of the freezer:
● *What temperature do you think the thermometer will show?*
● *What is the coldest temperature that you have ever heard of?*

EXTENSION
Try a few calculations: 'If the thermometer is on 3°C, and the temperature drops 5 degrees, where will the liquid come to?'

HOW MANY IN YOUR HAND?

†† *About six children sitting in a circle*
🕐 *About 10 minutes*

AIM
To count up to 10.

YOU WILL NEED
A tray holding enough Multilink cubes for each child to take a handful.

HOW TO PLAY
Go round the group, asking each child to take a handful of Multilink cubes. Then set a rule, such as 'The winner of the first game must have two red Multilink cubes. Have we a winner? Can you count your red cubes to check?'

In the second game choose a different rule, such as 'The winner must have three blue cubes.' Ask if there is a winner this time? Continue playing, changing the rule each time. After three games ask the children to replace their Multilink and take a fresh handful.

DISCUSSION QUESTIONS
- *How did you know you were the winner?*
- *Have we got more than one winner?*
- *Has anyone got more/less than two red cubes?*
- *Is there anyone who has no red cubes?*

TOWERS TO 10

†† *Up to ten children sitting round a table in pairs*
🕐 *About 10 minutes*

AIM
To count up to 10 and to match the numeral to the number of objects.

YOU WILL NEED
A supply of Multilink cubes, a set of cards numbered 1–10 for each child.

HOW TO PLAY
Give each child their set of cards and ask them to lay them out in order. The first pair of children to make Multilink towers to match all the numbers is the winner. (So the children will make separate Multilink towers with 2, then with 3, then with 4, and so on.) Extend the activity by discussing the towers.

DISCUSSION QUESTIONS
- *Which towers are taller than tower number 6?*
- *Which tower comes between tower 4 and tower 6? How do you know?*
- *Which towers are shorter than tower 4? How do you know? Can you show me how you know?*

ASSESSMENT
Look for children who are able to count the Multilink accurately.

POINT TO THE NUMBER

†† *Up to six children sitting round a table*
🕐 *About 15 minutes*

AIMS
To develop number recognition. To match the numeral to the count.

YOU WILL NEED
A set of cards numbered 1–5 for each child.

HOW TO PLAY
Give each child a set of number cards and ask them to lay out the cards in ascending order as quickly as possible. Then show, say, four fingers and ask the children to point quickly to the appropriate number on their cards. If the first child to point is correct he or she turns that number card over. The first child to turn over all his or her cards is the winner.

DISCUSSION QUESTIONS
- *How do you know that is the right card?*
- *Which number do you hope that I shall show next?*
- *Why do you want me to show you that number?*

DEVELOPING MENTAL MATHS

ASSESSMENT

Look for children who:
● are able to find the correct number card without counting their fingers;
● can point to the number without counting from the beginning.

HOW MANY DOTS?

†† *Up to six children sitting round a table*
🕐 *About 10 minutes*

AIM

To recognise dot patterns on a dice and match it to a written number.

YOU WILL NEED

A large spotted dice, a set of cards numbered 1–6 for each child, paper and pencils (optional).

HOW TO PLAY

Give each child a set of number cards and ask them to lay them out in ascending order. Then tell the children that when you throw the dice you want them to touch the card with the corresponding number as quickly as they can. The first child to point to the correct card turns it over. The winner is the first child to turn over all her or his cards.

DISCUSSION QUESTIONS

● *How do you know which card to turn over?*
● *What pattern do the five dots make? Can you draw it in the air/on paper?*

DO YOU HAVE PSYCHIC POWERS? If so then ring us on
* ******* *

ASSESSMENT

Look for children who:
● can identify the number of spots without counting;
● are able to point to the correct card quickly.

EXTENSION

Ask the children to lay out their cards in order and then turn them face down, still in order. Can the children turn over the correct card when you throw the dice?

BEAT OF THE DRUM

†† *Up to six children sitting round a table*
🕐 *About 10 minutes*

AIMS

To recognise that the last number is the size of the count. To develop strategies for checking a count.

YOU WILL NEED

A drum, a set of cards numbered 1–5 for each child.

HOW TO PLAY

Ask each child to lay out his or her cards in the correct order. Then tell the children to listen while you tap the drum and to count the number of taps in their minds. The first child to point to the corresponding card for the number of drum beats turns the card over. The first child to turn all their cards over is the winner.

Note: Matching counts to sounds is much harder than, say, observing the spots on a dice as there is nothing physical to check. (Consider how easy it is to lose count if you are counting clock chimes in the street.) Encourage the children to keep a 'tally' of the beats – for instance by using their fingers or by nodding.

DISCUSSION QUESTIONS

● *How do you know how many beats there were?*
● *How can we check? (Beat the drum again while saying simultaneously the number of beats.)*

ASSESSMENT

Look for children who:
● are able to count the taps correctly;
● can identify the number on the card without counting from the beginning.

EXTENSION

If children are able to count in 2s, play two drum beats close together to show that it is easier now to count in 2s.

COUNTING AND ORDERING

10S AND 1S

†† *Up to ten children sitting round a table*
🕐 *About 10 minutes*

AIM
To begin to recognise place value when counting in 10s.

YOU WILL NEED
A set of cards numbered 1–30, some counters, three 10p coins and nine 1p coins for each child.

HOW TO PLAY
Shuffle the number cards and place them face down in a pack on the floor. Turn over a card. Tell the child to use their coins to make the value shown. For example, if the number card was 27 the first child to make 27 with two 10p and seven 1p coins wins a counter. Continue playing until a child has won five counters to win the game.

DISCUSSION QUESTIONS
● *How many 10s and 1s will you need for this number?*
● *How do you know?*

ASSESSMENT QUESTIONS
● *Can the children read the numbers on the cards accurately?*
● *How quickly are they able to identify place value?*
● *Can the children count in 10s and 1s?*

EXTENSION
Try this game with bigger numbers, but use Deines' apparatus rather than coins.

CAN I FIT THEM IN?

†† *Up to ten children sitting round a table*
🕐 *About 15 minutes*

AIM
To make decisions when ordering numbers.

YOU WILL NEED
A set of 1–10 number cards, paper and pencil for each child, chalkboard.

HOW TO PLAY
Ask each child to draw five joined up squares on their paper.

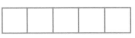

Explain to the children that you will be turning over the number cards and they have to choose in which boxes to write the numbers you reveal. Model the game on the board before beginning.

Draw the five squares. Then turn over a card, for example 4. Ask 'Where shall I write this number?' (Perhaps the second box.)

...., 4, ..., ..., ...,

Turn over the second card, for example 7. 'Where shall I write this number?'

...., 4, ..., ..., 7

The next card is 8. Can I write 8 in a square? No. Why? (Because you have written 7 in your last box and you cannot place it before that number.)

Continue until all the squares have been filled. The winner is the first player to write a number, in the correct order, in every square.

Discuss possible positions for the numbers. Non-consecutive series of numbers are fine: 2, 3, 5, 7, 9 for example.
● Which numbers would I expect to write in the middle square? Yes, number 5.
● Which numbers come before 5?
● Which number/numbers would I expect to write in the first square?

Play the game again and ask the children if they think they played a better game this time? Why?

Play five rounds before discussing the children's strategies.

DISCUSSION QUESTIONS
● *Why did you decide to put that number there?*
● *What numbers would it not be a good idea to put in the first square or two? Why not?*

EXTENSION
Try using ten squares and number cards 1–20. This game is more difficult. The children will need to have acquired more advanced skills in probability.

DEVELOPING MENTAL MATHS

LIFTS

✝✝ *Players in pairs (you may like to model the game with 16 children)*
🕐 *About 10 minutes to explain the game, then about 10 minutes for each pair to play it*

AIM
To understand that numbers go back beyond 0.

YOU WILL NEED
For each pair: a red dice, a blue dice, red and blue counters, cards numbered 0–10, about ten blank cards or pieces of paper, marker pen.

WHAT TO DO
Arrange the cards one above the other, from 0 up to 10. Explain that the cards represent the floors in a tall building: 0 is the ground floor and the other numbers are the floors above. Ask the children if they think there is anything below the ground floor of tall buildings. Once they agree that there might be lower floors – cellars and dungeons! – explain that together you are going to show these floors too. Place the blank cards underneath the 0 card, and ask the children what they think could be written on these cards. Some of the children may have seen negative numbers used in lifts (although they sometimes use letters such as 'B' for basement or 'LG' for lower ground floor) or on a thermometer. Write in –1 down to –10 on the cards.

Organise the children into pairs and tell each partner to take a different-coloured counter and to place them both on 0 (start). They then take turns to throw both dice together. The red dice takes the counters forwards and the blue dice takes them back. The winner is the first child to reach the 'deepest, darkest dungeon' at –10.

DISCUSSION QUESTIONS
● *Can you 'imagine' (predict) where your counter will land? Move it to check. (The children should be counting forwards/back in their heads.)*

● *How many floors are there between the dungeon (–1) and the room on floor 3?*

ASSESSMENT QUESTIONS
● *Do the children realise that they need small numbers on the red dice and large numbers on the blue dice in order to get to –10 quickly?*
● *Do they understand that when the two dice show the same number they can leave the counter in the same place?*
● *Are the children beginning to calculate where the counter will land without moving it?*

EXTENSIONS
● Extend your class number line to include negative numbers, and count into them regularly.
● Many children can relate to 'I owe you' notes: 'I owe Mummy 20p from next week's pocket money...', so the child has –20p.

UP OVER 100

✝✝ *Up to ten children sitting in a line on the carpet facing the teacher*
🕐 *About 10 minutes*

AIM
To read and write numbers greater than 100.

YOU WILL NEED
Multibase blocks, a supply of Multilink cubes, paper, pencil and a counter for each child.

HOW TO PLAY
Make a three-digit number with the Multibase, for example 234, and ask the children to write it down. Make two more three-digit numbers and ask the children to write these down also. Now ask them to put a counter on the biggest number they have written. The first child to do so, and be able to read the number correctly, wins a Multilink cube. Continue making sets of three numbers. The first child to make a ten-stick of Multilink wins.

DISCUSSION QUESTIONS
● *How do you know that number is the biggest?*
● *Which number has the smallest units number?*
● *Is the number with the most/any 9s the biggest number? Why not necessarily? (It depends on the position of the 9 within the number.)*

VARIATIONS
Use more counters and, for example, cover all the numbers >262, or numbers >200 but <400.

EXTENSION
Make numbers with a 0 as one of the digits. These are harder because of the empty 'column'.

STRATEGIES

CHILDREN SHOULD BE WORKING WITH NUMBERS OF THE ORDER:

RECEPTION/PRIMARY 1
● add or subtract two single-digit numbers.

YEAR 1/PRIMARY 2
● add a series of single-digit numbers to 20;
● add a single-digit number to any number (initially without crossing the 10);
● add 10 to any number;
● add a single-digit number to a multiple of 10;
● subtract a single-digit number from any number (initially without crossing the 10).

YEAR 2/PRIMARY 3
● add a series of single-digit numbers with a total of up to 50;
● add or subtract 10 or 100 to or from any number;
● add a multiple of 10 or 100 to any number (initially without moving to the next place value);
● add or subtract a single-digit number to a two-digit number;
● add two two-digit numbers < 50 crossing the 10s place as necessary.

AS A MINIMUM, BY THE END OF YEAR 2/PRIMARY 3 MOST CHILDREN SHOULD:

● be able to count on from any number without recounting the set;
● be able to add two two-digit numbers;
● know the complements to 10 (0 + 10, 1 + 9, 2 + 8, ... 10 + 0, and 10 – 0 = 10, 10 – 9 = 1 and so on);
● know and use addition and subtraction facts to 10 (1 + 2, 3 + 2, 4 + 2 and so on);
● know the double of any number to 10 + 10;
● know the half of any even number to 20;
● be able to add 10 or 100 to any number;
● recognise subtraction as the inverse of addition;
● understand that addition can be done in any order but subtraction cannot.

Many things can slow children down and stop them developing more effective methods. The most significant is a lack of known facts to draw upon. It is vital that children can tell a number story to explain the algorithm so that they can work out which strategy is needed. Eg 'There were fifteen greedy little pigs and six of them pushed the others away. How many were pushed away?'

STRATEGIES FOR ADDITION

Counting all: initially, children will need to have physical objects to count, later they will develop the ability to abstract the number names and count figural (or imagined objects). Encourage children to move from counting all to counting on, working with known facts wherever possible. Help a child move from counting all by allowing her or him to count out the two sets (say for 5 + 8) and put your hand over one set and ask, 'Do you need to recount these? How many are here? Can you count on from there? 5... 6... .' The first few times you do this a child may be unconvinced. Allow them to count to check.

Counting on: encourage children to add on from the larger set as this is more efficient:

for a set of three and a set of six, 'Six, 7, 8, 9' rather than 'Three, 4, 5, 6, 7, 8, 9'

Using doubles: learning doubles of single-digit numbers (such as: 1 + 1, 2 + 2 and so on) is valuable for using the 'near-doubles' or multiples of the doubles:

'I know that 5 + 5 is 10, so 5 + 6 is 10 + 1 = 11.'
'I know that 6 + 6 = 12, so 5 + 6 is 12 – 1 = 11.'
'I know that 5 + 5 = 10, so 50 + 50 = 100.'

Addition (and subtraction) bonds to 10 should be available to the child for instant recall and use: a part of the solution to a problem or the multiple of a number bond might be spotted:

'I know that 6 + 4 = 10, so 60 + 40 = 100
Also that 16 + 4 = 20, 26 + 4 = 30'

Making a link with subtraction

10 − 4 = 6, 20 − 4 = 16
100 − 40 = 60, 100 − 99 = 1, 100 − ? = 90

Bridging through 10 or 20 builds upon the number facts to 10 or 20 and the fact that it is easier to deal with single digits or multiples of 10:

'I know 8 + 2 = 10 so 8 + 4 = 10 + 2 = 12'
'I know 7 + 3 = 10 so 17 + 3 = 20'
'I know 6 + 4 = 10 so 16 + 5 = 20 + 1'
Solves 17 + 6 as 17 + 3 = 20, 20 + 3 = 23

Partitioning uses place value and may involve the creation of another 10:

14 + 8; 10 + 8 + 4 = 10 + 10 + 2 = 22
24 + 18; 20 + 10 + 8 + 4 = 30 + 8 + 4 =
30 + 10 + 2 = 42

STRATEGIES FOR SUBTRACTION

Counting on and back: initially children model subtraction by 'putting away' fingers or removing items from a collection. They need to be encouraged to move on to counting back or counting on.

To solve 5 − 3:

● count back by saying three counting words, keep track by using fingers saying 'Five, 4 (put up one finger), 3 (put up second finger), 2 (put up third finger) – the answer is 2';
● count on by counting from the smaller number to the larger number and keep track of the number of counting words on fingers, saying 'Three, 4 (puts up one finger), 5 (puts up second finger) – the answer is 2'.

Using known facts: including doubles

Solves 10 − 3 with the knowledge that
7 + 3 = 10
Solves 20 − 4 with the knowledge that
16 + 4 = 20
Also solves 9 − 4 with the knowledge that
4 + 4 = 8

Compensating:

Solves 20 − 9 as 20 − 10 + 1

Partitioning into 10s and 1s uses knowledge of place value:

47 − 35 (40 − 30) + (7 − 5)

Bridging back through 10 uses knowledge of addition facts:

35 − 17 the child knows 7 = 5 + 2 and
reasons that
35 − 10 = 25, 25 − 5 = 20, 20 − 2 = 18

Complementary addition
(or 'Shopkeeper's addition'):

64 − 27   27 + 3 = 30
+ 30 = 60
+ 4 = 64
and altogether I added 37 so 64 − 27 = 37

PUT THE NUMBER IN YOUR HEAD

†† *About ten children and the teacher sitting in a circle (it may be necessary to put younger or less able children near the beginning of the count)*
🕐 *About 5 minutes*

AIM
To demonstrate and encourage counting on from any number.

YOU WILL NEED
Plastic cubes (optional).

WHAT TO DO
Ask each child to take three cubes or to show three fingers. Begin the count by placing one hand on your head and saying 'Nought and count on 3: 0, 1, 2, 3', as each finger is folded or each cube touched. Continue around the circle with each child adding on 3. Repeat the activity, beginning at another place in the circle.

DISCUSSION QUESTIONS
● *What do you think the next number will be?*
● *Can you find it on the number line?*

EXTENSIONS
● Encourage the children to whisper the first two numbers of their count: 'One, 2, **3**; 4, 5, **6**.'
● Write the numbers on the board. Ask 'Can you read the numbers? Can you see them on the number line? How many numbers are there in between?'

● Once the children are confident with counting on, encourage counting back. Ensure that you have counted around the circle in order to establish the total. The child beginning the count puts the number in his head and says, 'Thirty-three', raises three fingers and folds them down one at a time saying '30, 31, 30.' The next child 'puts 30 in her head' and uses three fingers to count back from 29. Continue round the circle.

BEARS ON THE FLOOR

†† *Whole class sitting in a semicircle with the teacher sitting in the space*
🕐 *About 5 minutes*

AIM
To begin to develop a strategy for counting on.

YOU WILL NEED
Plastic counting bears (or cubes or counters).

WHAT TO DO
Place four plastic bears on the carpet and ask the children to show you the number of bears with their fingers. Add two more bears and again ask the children to show you the new number with their fingers. Ask them how they know. Encourage the children to keep the first number in their head and to count on.

You may need to model the answer by placing your hand over the four bears and saying, 'Four add one is five, add another one is six – six bears.' Demonstrate with your fingers. Show four, raise one more and say 'Five', then another while saying 'Six'. Repeat with the children joining in.

DISCUSSION QUESTIONS
● *Think of the bears on the carpet. How do you know that number of fingers is two more?*
● *Did you need to count the bears on the carpet again?*

VARIATIONS
Add a different amount. Place a sheet of paper over the (four) bears and put (three) more bears on the floor. Again ask the children to show you (with their fingers or on a number line) the total number of bears. If you began with the same number of bears, did the children need to count the bears on the carpet this time? Why/why not? If necessary, model the answers to encourage counting on or using number bonds by placing your hand on the paper and saying 'Four'. Then point to each bear and raise one finger at a time as you say 'Five, six, seven bears altogether'.

DOUBLING BEARS

†† *Whole class sitting in a semicircle with a teacher in the space*
⏱ *About 10 minutes*

AIMS
To demonstrate and learn doubles (up to 10 + 10) as an aid to addition. To introduce the vocabulary associated with doubling.

YOU WILL NEED
Plastic bears (or cubes), two sets of hoops or rings.

WHAT TO DO
Place a bear (or cube) in one of the hoops and ask the children how many bears there will be if you put one bear in the other hoop. Let a child demonstrate and give you the answer 'Two'. Emphasise to the children, 'One bear and one more makes two bears'.

Then place both bears in one hoop and ask how many bears there will be altogether if you put the same number of bears in the other hoop. Again, ask a child to demonstrate and emphasise that two bears and two bears makes four bears. Continue adding bears and matching the hoops up to 10 + 10.

DISCUSSION QUESTIONS
● *How many bears do I need to match the other hoop?*
● *How many bears is that altogether?*
● *Do you need to count all the bears or can you count on?*
How could we remember that 3 + 3 = 6? Hopefully the children are beginning to remember the chant and count on in 2s. 1 + 1 = 2, 2 + 2 = 4, 3 + 3 = 6.

EXTENSIONS
● It is useful for the children to have automatic recall of these number facts. Reinforce them using a chant and a finger game. Using both hands, touch your fingers and say 'One and one is two, two and two is four... five and five is ten.'
● Write the number sentences on the board and ask the children to read them with you. If children know that 3 + 3 = 6, what do they think 30 + 30 might be? Or 300 + 300, or 3000 + 3000?
● To reinforce halving, give the children a total number of bears and ask them how many you should put in each ring. 'If I've got ten bears to put in the two hoops, how many will go in each one?'
● As a finger game, put the fingers of both hands together and say, 'Five and five is ten. Ten fingers take away five leaves five' and move one hand away. Continue with 8 – 4, 6 – 3, 4 – 2, 2 – 1.

FINGER NUMBER BONDS

†† *Whole class facing the teacher*
⏱ *Two or three minutes twice a week until the children are quick and confident*

AIMS
To learn and develop quick recall of addition bonds up to 10 + 10.

WHAT TO DO
Ask the children to use their fingers to show you the numbers up to 10. (See the counting activity, 'Keep fit maths' on page 13.) Then encourage them to use their fingers to follow as you say the words: '0 and 10 make 10, 1 and 9 make 10, 2 and 8 make 10...'. Continue until 10 and nothing.

If the children do not spot the pattern, point out how the numbers on the left get one bigger each time and the ones on the right get smaller.

DISCUSSION QUESTIONS
● *Can you hear a pattern? Can you explain it?*
● *Why do you think this pattern occurs?*
Write the number sentences on the board and ask:
● *Is the pattern clearer now?*
Show the children four fingers:
● *How many fingers am I showing on this hand?*
● *How do you know how many I am hiding?*

EXTENSION
If each finger stands for 10 (or 100), discuss how many the children can show with their hands. Repeat the discussion given above until the children are confident.

ADDITION AND SUBTRACTION

BEADS TO 10

†† About 15 children facing the teacher
🕐 About 5 minutes

AIMS

To develop counting on to 10. To reinforce number bonds up to 10.

YOU WILL NEED

Ten large round or cubed beads threaded on a lace or piece of string and tied at both ends with about 5cm of play.

WHAT TO DO

Hold up the beads (if possible arrange them in alternating colours as this will help you to keep count) and ask the children to help you count them. Count together, touching and moving the beads, to establish the total.

Ask the children if the number will be the same if you count the other way. (You may need to do this if the children are in doubt.)

Then tell the children that you want them to count silently the beads that you are showing. Move, for example, four beads, carefully and slowly, retaining the six in the palm of your hand. Can the children tell you how many beads you have moved and how many you are hiding? How do they know?

If necessary, model the answer by saying 'Four showing' and '1, 2, 3, 4, 5, 6 hiding in my hand. That's four count on six.' Hold the four beads and then move the six beads along, counting aloud together '5, 6, 7, 8, 9, 10'.

DISCUSSION QUESTIONS

● *Why will the number be the same if we count the beads the other way?*
● *How do you know how many beads I am hiding? Did anyone work it out in a different way?*
If you have used beads in alternating colours:
● *Do you know if the next number will be odd or even? (Odds will all be one colour, evens the other.)*

VARIATION

● Try this activity using a different number of beads.

PAIRS TO MAKE 10

†† *Twelve children sitting in a circle*
🕐 *10 minutes*

AIM

To reinforce number bonds to 10.

YOU WILL NEED

Twelve cards. Each card should have a different number of spots from 0–10, include two cards which have five spots.

WHAT TO DO

Shuffle the cards and deal them out, one for each child. Ask the children to read their cards and place them face up on the carpet. Explain that you would like each child to find a partner 'to make 10' and then sit down in a circle. When they have done this, each pair should read out their card values and their total. Collect, shuffle and redistribute the cards and play again.

DISCUSSION QUESTIONS

● *How did you know Sally was your partner, Abena?*
● *Did anyone find his or her partner in another way?*
● *Can anyone think of a way of always knowing which number is missing?*

EXTENSIONS

● After the game, suggest arranging the cards in paired order, 0 + 10, 1 + 9 and so on, in the centre of the circle. Read the pattern of the cards with the group. Tell one child to turn away from the circle while another child turns one of the cards over. The first child turns back and must say the value of the card that has been turned over, turning it face up again to check. Continue round the circle until each child has taken part.
● Use numbered cards instead of cards with spots on them.

DISCUSSION QUESTIONS
● *Can anyone write a number sentence to show what we have done?*
● *Can anyone tell a number story about the sentence 33 + 20 = 53?*

EXTENSION
Explore subtraction in the same way. Ask 'What will the answer be if I take away 20?' Go on to add or take away units.

DOUBLING THE 10S

†† *Whole class facing the teacher*
🕐 *5 minutes*

AIM
To demonstrate and learn doubles up to 50 + 50 as an aid to addition and subtraction.

WHAT TO DO
(You may like to refer to the activity 'Doubling bears', on page 33.)

Ask the children to imagine that each finger is worth 10. Raise one finger at a time and count up to 50 on one hand and then up to 50 on the other. Ask the children to put both thumbs together and say '10 add 10 makes 20'. Continue with the other fingers up to 50 add 50.

Go on to halve the numbers. Place all your fingers together and say '100'. Remove one hand and say 'Half of 100 is 50' and/or '100 take away 50 leaves 50.' Write, or ask the children to write, the number sentences involved on the board:

$$10 + 10 = 20, 20 - 10 = 10$$
$$20 + 20 = 40, 40 - 20 = 20$$
$$...50 + 50 = 100, 100 - 50 = 50$$

ADDING 10S

†† *Whole class sitting in a semicircle with teacher in the space*
🕐 *10 minutes*

AIM
To develop counting on in 10s from any number.

YOU WILL NEED
Multibase tens and unit cubes, a large sheet of paper, paper, pencils.

WHAT TO DO
Pick out three tens and three ones from the Multibase and place them on the carpet. Ask the children to write down the number on their pieces of paper. Choose one child to come and write the number on your large sheet and read it out. Ask another child to count the bricks to check the answer. With the class, re-count the bricks, encouraging the children to join in – '10, 20, 30, 31, 32, 33'.

Refer to the number written on your large sheet of paper and remind the children that 33 is three 10s and three 1s. Ask the children to imagine what the number will be if you add two more 10s, and tell them to write down this new number on their pieces of paper. Ask another child to write the new number on your large sheet. 'Does everyone agree? Who can add the two 10s and read the answer? Which number has changed? Why?'

Model the answer by placing your hand over the thirty three and saying '33, count on ten is 43, count on another ten is 53'.

DISCUSSION QUESTIONS
● *Can anyone do the doubling without using their fingers?*
● *What do you see in your mind when you are doing this?*
Looking at the number sentences on the board:
● *Can you see any patterns?*
● *Can you explain the patterns?*

EXTENSIONS
● Set challenges such as, 'If I know 1 + 1 = 2 and 10 + 10 = 20, what will 100 + 100 be? Or half of 8000?'

● Investigate halving 'odd' numbers of 10s or 100s, such as 30, 50 and so on.

FIND THE TOTAL

†† *About ten children sitting in a semicircle*
⏱ *About 10 minutes*

AIM
To use a variety of addition strategies to make a two-digit total.

YOU WILL NEED
Cards numbered 0 to your chosen total, a calculator.

WHAT TO DO
(In this example, the chosen total is 26. To choose suitable values, refer to the section on 'Strategies', pages 30–31, 'Children should be working with numbers of the order...'.)

Spread out the cards face up in the space. Ask the children to look for two cards that make 26. Go round the circle, making sure that each child is given sufficient time to think and answer. Ask one child to use a calculator to check the answers.

DISCUSSION QUESTIONS
● *Can all the cards be used?*
● *How do you know that those two cards total 26?*
● *Are there any cards left? Why? Which card is needed to make it into 26? (13, because 13 has no bond – its double – in the set.)*

EXTENSION
Use cards suitable for bigger totals, such as 50 or 100.

ADDITION AND SUBTRACTION

MAKING A 0-NUMBER

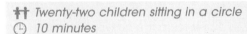

†† *Twenty-two children sitting in a circle*
⏱ *10 minutes*

AIMS
To add a single digit to a two-digit number. To extend the use of number bonds to 10 to make multiples of 10.

YOU WILL NEED
Cards numbered 20–30 and a set numbered 0–10.

WHAT TO DO
Shuffle the cards and deal them out, one per child. Tell the children that they must move round and find a partner to make their cards total 30. They must first listen carefully while they each read out the number on their card, and then find an appropriate partner. When they have done this, each pair should read out their sum, for example 21 + 9 = 30, to check they have matched up correctly.

DISCUSSION QUESTIONS
● *How did you find out that Clare is your partner?*
● *Did anyone work it out in a different way?*
● *Can you write down a number sentence to show your sum?*

EXTENSION
● Use cards from 20–50 with a 0–10 set. Hold up a card, for instance 40, and ask which number could be added to this to give a total of 50. Encourage the children to think systematically by using their knowledge of number bonds. 'I'm 24 so I need someone with a 6 because I know that 4 + 6 makes a nought number'.

DICE TAKE AWAY

†† *15 children sitting in a semicircle with the teacher in the space*
🕐 *10 minutes*

AIM
To develop subtraction bonds using knowledge of addition bonds to 10.

YOU WILL NEED
Several sticks of Multilink with ten cubes in each stick, two large dice (cover each number 6 with a 0, alternatively you could use a 0–10 spinner, or a polyhedral dice), paper, pencils.

WHAT TO DO
Place four ten-sticks of Multilink on the carpet and ask the children to write down the number they represent (the number of cubes). Throw the two dice, and ask the children to total them mentally and then take this number away from the Multilink total. They should then write down the new number. Discuss how the children found their answers. Ask a child to remove the dice total from the Multilink and count to check the answer.

DISCUSSION QUESTIONS
● *How many Multilink will be left? How did you get that answer?*
● *Which is the quickest way? Why?*
● *What will the answer always include if we take 4 away from a 0-number?*
● *Why?*
   It is important to rehearse all the subtraction number bonds from a nought number: 10 – 1 = 9, 20 – 1= 19, 30 – 1= 29.

VARIATION
For younger or less able children, use only one dice so they do not have to do addition and subtraction in the same calculation. (You will not need to blank out the 6 in this case.) Using the spinner or polyhedral dice provides larger numbers to subtract, without the need for the children to do the addition in the middle, which some pupils may find unnecessarily complicated at first.

EXTENSION
Put out Multilink to represent other two-digit numbers, for example 34 or 29, and then continue as before.

10S AND 1S TAKE-AWAY

†† *15 children sitting in a semicircle*
🕐 *10 minutes*

AIM
To develop strategies for subtracting 10s and 1s.

YOU WILL NEED
Cards numbered with the 10s, from 10 to 100, a card with a number 1, two cards with the subtraction sign, a large sheet of paper, a felt-tipped pen.

WHAT TO DO
Lay out the five cards to face the children in this order:

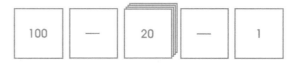

(100, the subtraction sign, all the other tens numbers in order – or shuffled – in a pile, the subtraction sign, the number 1 card.)

   Ask the children to help you read the problem, for example '100 take away 20 take away 1 is …?' Let the children take turns to write the answer on the sheet. When they have done this they should remove a card from the tens pile to reveal the next problem.

DISCUSSION QUESTIONS
● *Is there a pattern to the answers?*
● *What is the pattern?*
● *Who can explain why this pattern has appeared?*
● *What would happen if you took away the 1 first?*
● *In which order is it easier to do the subtraction and why?*
● *What happens to the 10s digit when you take away the 1? (The 10s digit always goes down by 1 as you bridge back into the previous decade.)*
● *Can you show these steps on the number line?*

ASSESSMENT
How could I work out 100 – 51?

VARIATIONS
● Use a different unit number.
● Use a different 10s number, rather than 100, to begin the problem.

EXTENSION
Use a pile of mixed tens and units.

DEVELOPING MENTAL MATHS

ADDITION AND SUBTRACTION

HOW MUCH MONEY DID YOUR STALL MAKE?

†† *About 10 children working in pairs*

🕐 *About 20 minutes*

AIMS

To count money in a systematic way. To order the amounts and find differences.

YOU WILL NEED

One container for each pair labelled with a stall name, each containing a sum of money, paper and pencils, a marker pen, a large sheet of paper listing all the stall names, for example 'Cakes', 'Books', 'White elephant', 'Bottle', 'Tombola' and so on.

WHAT TO DO

Give each pair one of the labelled containers with a suitable amount of money appropriate to their ability (see the section on 'Strategies' on pages 30–31). Ask each pair to count up how much money 'their' stall raised and then to enter the total on the chart. Tell them that you will be returning later to see how they counted their total so that it can be checked.

When all the pairs have written up their totals, gather the children together and discuss how they counted their money and worked out the total. (You may find this activity is best applied to a real classroom scenario, such as counting money from a charity collection or for a class journey.)

DISCUSSION QUESTIONS

● *Can anyone explain how they counted their money? Which methods were most successful? Why?*

● *Can you explain how you recorded the total?*

● *How are the pounds and pence separated?*

● *Can we write the amounts in order? Which stall raised most money? How do you know?*

● *How many stalls raised more/less money than your stall?*

● *What is the difference between your total and the largest amount raised?*

● *How much money was raised altogether?*

● *How many stalls raised more/less than £10?*

ASSESSMENT

Look for whether the children were systematic, and how they arranged their coins for counting.

TELLING STORIES: 1

†† *Whole class sitting facing the teacher*

🕐 *Approximately 5 minutes each day*

AIM

To model the maths in stories, focusing on addition and subtraction.

WHAT TO DO

Ask the children to model numbers with their hands in response to a story. For example, 'There were four little birds sitting on a branch, when one more little bird flew down. How many little birds are there now?' Observe the children's hands to check whether they have given the correct response.

If the children are hesitant, repeat the story and model the answer, making sure that the children are joining in.

Write number sentences to reflect the stories: $4 + 1 = 5$.

Note: It is important to vary the position of the unknown quantity: $? + 7 = 10$ or $10 - ? = 4$, for example.

Encourage the children to be aware that subtraction is the inverse of addition by asking, 'If one little bird flies away, how many little birds will be left?'

These story ideas can become more complicated as the children become more confident with numbers up to 20. The children can use their hands and feet to solve these problems. For example, 15 birds are sitting on the fence (ten toes and five fingers), 13 fly away. How many are left? (The children can take ten toes away first, then three fingers.)

DISCUSSION QUESTIONS
● *What number sentence could we write to tell this story?*
● *Who can tell us a story to go with this number sentence?*
Write on the board an example such as 3 + 3 = 6.

ASSESSMENT
Tell the children to put their hands behind their backs. Then tell them a longer, more involved story which they have to keep track of without looking at their hands. For instance, 'Six birds are on the tree, two fly away, three come back. How many birds are on the tree now?'

EXTENSION
Discuss an example, such as 'If I know that 4 + 1 = 5, what else do I know?' Write up their suggestions: 1 + 4 = 5, 5 – 1 = 4, 5 – 4 = 1, 40 + 10 = 50 and so on.

HOW FEW?

†† *Whole class explanation round the chalkboard, investigation in pairs*
🕐 *About 10 minutes*

AIM
To investigate using coins to solve addition problems.

YOU WILL NEED
Paper, pencils, a supply of coins of different denominations, chalkboard.

WHAT TO DO
Pose the children a problem such as 'I have a pocket full of coins, but no pound coins. Which coins could I use to pay for this 99p book? What is the least number of coins I would need?'

Let one child choose some coins to make 99p and write their values on the board, for example, 50p, 20p, 10p, 10p, 5p, 2p, 1p and 1p.

Discuss how many coins have been used. Then say something such as 'This has given us a very good start, can anyone combine/exchange any of the coins so that we have fewer? Could we swap the two 10p coins for a 20p coin?' If the children agree, cross out the two 10p coins and write 20p instead. Continue until the least number of coins has been found.

Write some more sums of money on the board and ask the children to investigate with the money the least number of coins needed for that amount.

Follow up by bringing the children together in a large circle on the carpet and asking them to share their ideas in turn. Some children may

suggest using only one of their coins and expecting change. For example, the least number of coins to pay for a 47p item might be a 50p with a 2p and a 1p back in change or two 20p coins, a 5p and a 2p.

DISCUSSION QUESTIONS
● *Who thinks they worked systematically?*
● *Why do you think that?*
● *Can you explain to us how you worked out the number of coins?*

EXTENSIONS
● If I can only use four coins what amounts can I make? The children should look at the various combinations.
● Extend to prices larger than £1. You may need to discuss the convention for separating pounds from pence.

SCHOOL SPRING SALE

†† *About 15 children sitting in a semicircle facing the list*
🕐 *About 15 minutes*

AIMS
To develop strategies for adding. To count on ('shopkeeper's addition') to find change.

YOU WILL NEED
A pre-prepared price list, as shown here. (You can add further items to this list if you wish.)

Books	15p each
Comics	5p each
Posters	50p each
Toy cars	25p each

WHAT TO DO
Show the children the list. Ask them to imagine that they each have £1 to spend at a sale. Ask them what they would buy. They will probably find

that they have two choices. The children can buy more than one book or comic and so on, or they may wish to buy a few items and keep change for something else. Write their choices on the board and then discuss them.

DISCUSSION QUESTIONS
● *Which choices used all the money?*
● *Which choices give change?*
● *How much would the change be? How did you work out the change?*
● *Did anyone overspend? What would you do if you overspent at the School Spring Sale? How much would you need to borrow?*
● *How much would it cost to buy one of each item?*
● *Who can explain their method of totalling?*
● *How many toy cars can I buy for £1?*
● *Can I use all my money if I only buy books?*

EXTENSION
Develop the price list to include bigger numbers: 35p, 25p, 90p and 65p respectively.

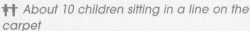

NEARLY 10

✚✚ *About 10 children sitting in a line on the carpet*
🕐 *About 10 minutes*

AIM
To encourage the children to use a variety of strategies to add on or subtract numbers that are nearly 10.

YOU WILL NEED
Enough 0–9 number cards for each child to have three cards, chalkboard.

WHAT TO DO
Shuffle the number cards and give each child three cards. Ask the children to each make a three-digit number with their cards and then to write their numbers on the board in order.

Ask each child to add 10, in their heads, to one of the numbers on the chalkboard. (They should not add it to their own number.) Then ask the child to tell the class the new number. Where do the children think this new number should be written in the order on the board? Are they sure this is the right place? How do they know?

Look at the numbers together. Encourage the children to think very carefully to see if they know what has happened. Move on to considering adding or subtracting 11 or 9 each time instead of 10.

DISCUSSION QUESTIONS
● *Imagine what would happen if we added 11 to every number. Who can explain their answer?*
● *Did anyone use another method?*
● *Is there a pattern when 11 is added to these numbers? Can this pattern be used for checking our answer?*

ASSESSMENT QUESTIONS
● *Can the children use their knowledge of number bonds in a variety of situations to help calculate quickly?*
● *Can the children use this knowledge to bridge across the 10s?*

EXTENSIONS
● How can we add 12 to these numbers very quickly?
● What about taking away 9? (Do not choose numbers that bridge across the hundreds at first.) How can we find the answer? Is there a quick way? How can we check that the answer is right?

HOW TO MAKE 10

†† *About 10 children sitting at tables in pairs*
🕐 *About 10 minutes*

AIM
To find the number bonds for 10.

YOU WILL NEED
A supply of counting cubes, paper and pencils, a copy of photocopiable page 64 for each child (optional).

WHAT TO DO
Organise the children into pairs and ask each pair to take ten cubes and put them into two piles. Let each pair have a turn at describing their piles of cubes as a number sentence, for example 'Six and four makes ten'.

The children could reflect further on this investigation by using the writing frame on photocopiable page 64.

DISCUSSION QUESTIONS
● *Can you write down all the different number sentences you can make? (The children may need to reorder their piles before recording their number sentences.)*
● *Are there any that we haven't written?*
● *Can we reorder and rewrite them to make a pattern? Which number sentence shall we write first?*
After writing two or three, ask:
● *Can you see the pattern?*
● *What do you think will come next? Why?*
Continue until all the various combinations have been written.

EXTENSIONS
● Encourage the children to reflect on *all* the knowledge they have. For example, if they know that 3 + 7 = 10, remind them that 7 + 3 = 10 too, and that 10 – 7 = 3 and 10 – 3 = 7.
● Let the children work with larger numbers of cubes to find, for example, the combinations that can be used to make 20.
● Use Base 10 longs and ask the children to make the 0 to 100 pattern: 0 + 100 = 100; 10 + 90 = 100; 20 + 80 = 100... Ask the children 'Does this pattern remind you of another pattern?'
The children need to be reminded that they can apply this knowledge to solve other problems:
? + 40 = 100; 60 + ? = 100; 100 – 60 = ?; 100 – 40 = ?; 100 – ? = 40; 100 – 0 = 100.

HOW MANY WAYS CAN YOU MAKE 7P?

†† *About 10 children working in pairs on the carpet*
🕐 *About 10 minutes*

AIM
To investigate making a given total.

YOU WILL NEED
Cubes, counters or plastic shapes such as bears, a supply of money, a copy of photocopiable page 64 for each child (optional).

WHAT TO DO
Tell the children that the bears cost 7p today. Which combination of coins could they use to buy a teddy?

Organise the children into pairs and ask them to buy a bear with 7p. How many different ways can they buy a 7p bear. Ask each pair to show you a different way to buy the teddies. When each pair has placed their teddy and coins on the carpet, encourage the children to place the bears and coins in this pattern:

> 1p, 1p, 1p, 1p, 1p, 1p, 1p.
> 2p, 1p, 1p 1p, 1p, 1p.
> 2p, 2p, 1p, 1p, 1p...
> 5p, 2p.

It is important to spend time modelling the investigation. This gives the children strategies for investigating on their own and encourages them to be systematic. Encourage further thought by giving the children photocopiable page 64.

DISCUSSION QUESTIONS
● *Has anyone got any other ways of making 7p? (10p with 3p change, perhaps!)*
● *How can we check that we have all the ways of making 7p?*
● *Which way shall we place the coins first? (You may like to suggest seven 1p coins, or 5p and 2p as it is most efficient/uses least coins.)*
● *What comes next?*
● *How many different ways are there?*
● *How can we be systematic?*

EXTENSION
Try totals of 20p, 50p or £1, and/or limit the coins to only 'silver' or 'bronze', or to a maximum number of coins, for example 15.

TWENTY

† About 10 children working in pairs on the carpet
⏱ About 10 minutes

AIMS
To extend knowledge of number bonds to 10. To recognise or work out number bonds to 20.

YOU WILL NEED
A set of 0–19 number cards (include two cards for 10) for each pair, paper, pencils, a copy of photocopiable page 64 for each child (optional).

WHAT TO DO
Give each pair their set of number cards and ask them to find all the pairs of cards that make 20 and to write down the different combinations. Ask them to try and arrange the answers 'in a pattern' (systematically). If necessary, encourage the children to use what they know about pairs of numbers that make 10 to inform their finding of pairs of numbers that make 20. Encourage the children to reflect on their work by using the writing frame given on photocopiable page 64.

DISCUSSION QUESTIONS
● *Was anyone able to arrange their numbers 'in a pattern'/systematically?*
● *Can you explain how you worked?*
● *How is the pattern like the one for making 10?*
● *Can you write your first pair of numbers in a number sentence on the board? (For example, 20 + 0 = 20, or 0 + 20 = 20.)*
● *Who can write what comes next? (19 + 1 = 20, or 1 + 19 = 20.) Why do you think that is the next one?*

ONE POTATO...

† Whole class working in pairs
⏱ About 15 minutes

AIM
To explore ways of making a given answer by adding or subtracting.

YOU WILL NEED
Paper, pencils, chalkboard, a copy of photocopiable page 64 for each child (optional). Less able children may need counting apparatus.

WHAT TO DO
Write a number on the board, for example 27. Tell the children to imagine that you have 27 potatoes and ask them in how many different ways you can arrange them into two piles. Write some

suggestions on the board and try them out, for example, 20 + 7, 10 + 17, 1 + 26 and so on.

Ask the children to work in pairs and to write down at least 15 different ways that the piles could be organised. Give them about 10 minutes to work on this and then gather the class together and share their ideas. You may like to set a different target number to younger or less able children.

Follow up by asking the children to gather round the board. Ask each pair of children to give you a different combination. (It is often best to begin with less confident children.) If any children suggest 20 + 7 and 7 + 20, for example, query whether these two sums are the same. (Yes, in this case because they are all the same potatoes.) The children may like to write up their investigations on the frame on photocopiable page 64.

DISCUSSION QUESTIONS
● *How did you decide to split the potatoes into piles?*
● *Have we found all the ways of splitting the potatoes into piles?*
● *What did you see in your mind when splitting up the potatoes?*
● *Can you write a number sentence to describe what you did?*
● *Did you use 'take away' or 'add' first?*

EXTENSIONS
● Move on to working with a different number of potatoes, for example up to 50, then 100 or more and ask the children to divide these into two.
● In how many ways can the children arrange the 27 potatoes into three piles? Ask them what strategies they used to tackle this. Encourage them to work systematically and to exchange strategies for organising their work. Again, move on to use bigger numbers as the children's confidence increases.

FIND THE 7S

†† *About 6 children, sitting in a circle, on the carpet*
🕐 *About 10 minutes*

AIM
To encourage counting on (or other addition strategies).

YOU WILL NEED
A box of dominoes.

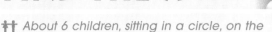

HOW TO PLAY
This is a very basic game to help young children move from counting to calculation.

Ask the children to spread the dominoes on the floor face down, taking turns to pick up one domino. If the dots total 7, the child can keep the domino. If not it is put back. Let them keep taking turns until all the 7-dominoes have been removed. The winner is the child with the most dominoes.

DISCUSSION QUESTIONS
● *Do the dots on your domino add up to 7?*
● *How did you find out the total number of dots?*
● *Would anyone have counted differently?*
● *Do you know how many spots there are in any of the patterns (for example, 2, 3 or 5)? Do you need to count those?*

ASSESSMENT
Look for children beginning to count on, who are able to recognise patterns without counting them (for instance they know the pattern of six dots and so on), or can recognise the doubles.

EXTENSIONS
● To move on to number bonds up to 10, use 12 cards, each with a different number of spots from 0–10 and including two cards with five spots.
● Throw two polyhedral dice and find the total score each time. A child wins a counter for each total score of 13, for example. The first child to collect a given number of counters wins.

DICE BINGO

†† *Children sitting in a wide semicircle*
🕐 *About ten minutes*

AIM
To develop familiarity with number pairs.

YOU WILL NEED
Two large spotted dice, chalkboard, paper and pencils.

HOW TO PLAY
Using the two dice, ask the children what the smallest total they can make is and then the largest. Let them use the dice to demonstrate.

In response to the children's answers, write 2 and 12 at the top and bottom of the board. Then encourage the children to make the numbers in-between. Work through each number with the children, asking them to find that total by turning the dice.

Next ask the children to choose four of the numbers from the board and to write these on their pieces of paper. Throw the two dice and ask the children to find the total quietly in their heads. (You may want to encourage counting on, or remind the children to 'put the big number in your head and count on'.) Ask a child to give the answer and explain how she or he found it.

This number is then crossed off on the board. Children who chose it also cross it out on their pieces of paper. The first child to cross out all of her or his numbers and shout 'Bingo' is the winner. Check by referring to the board. The children then choose four more numbers and play again.

DISCUSSION QUESTIONS
● *Can you show us how you know that is the smallest total? And the largest?*
● *Why do some numbers come up more often than others?*
● *Which numbers are easy to find? Why?*

VARIATION
If you allow subtraction of pairs, then 1 can be made as 2 – 1, 3 – 2 and so on, as well as making available other ways of finding the numbers from 2 to 5.

EXTENSION
This game can be adapted to use lots of different number generators, totals and even operations. Try a numbered 7–12 dice with the 1–6 spotted dice, or two 7–12 dice, or combinations involving 1–12 polyhedral dice, or a blank six-sided dice marked 10–60 with another marked with single digits.

ADDITION AND SUBTRACTION

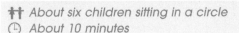

HOW MANY MORE?

✝ *About six children sitting in a circle*
🕐 *About 10 minutes*

AIM
To add on up to 10.

YOU WILL NEED
A 1–6 dice, some counters.

HOW TO PLAY
Tell the children that you will be throwing the dice and you would like them to show you how many more are needed in order to make 10. The first child to show the difference each time, with his or her fingers for example, is the winner of that round and receives a counter. The winner of the game is the first child to get five counters.

DISCUSSION QUESTIONS
● *Who is counting from 1 each time? Do you think you could try to count on? Let's try together.*
● *Is counting on quicker than counting from 1?*
● *Does anyone know how many fingers to show without counting on?*
● *Which numbers are easy? Which are hard?*
● *Can anyone say the sum we have made (for example, 6 on the dice add on 4 is 10)?*

ASSESSMENT
Look for children counting on and remembering to stop at 10. Hopefully, some children will be starting to use their knowledge of number bonds at this stage.

MORE THAN 10

✝ *About six children sitting in a circle*
🕐 *About 10 minutes*

AIM
To add on from 10.

YOU WILL NEED
One 10p coin, nine 1p coins, paper, pencils.

HOW TO PLAY
Ask each child to write down secretly four numbers between 10 and 19.

Place the 10p and a few 1p coins on the carpet. Allow the children a short time to total the coins and explain that you would like them to cross out that number if they have written it on their paper.

Continue with different coin combinations until someone has crossed out all her or his numbers and is the winner.

DISCUSSION QUESTION
Do you have to count all the coins every time?

ASSESSMENT QUESTION
Are the children counting on or are they using number facts?
Look for children who can identify the answer, without re-counting. For example, if you added or subtracted 1p from the last total.

EXTENSION
Play a similar game with more coins to extend the numbers to 50 or 100. Alternatively, use Deines' apparatus and include hundreds, tens and units. It is much harder to play this game with numbers including a 0, such as 102. Encourage the children to start from the larger number and to count on.

FIRST TO 20

✝ *About ten children sitting in a circle in pairs*
🕐 *About 10 minutes*

AIM
To use addition and subtraction to make a given total.

YOU WILL NEED
A numbered dice for each pair, paper, pencil.

HOW TO PLAY
Arrange the children into pairs and tell them to take turns to throw the dice and keep a running total on their paper. The first pair to total exactly 20 are the winners. Allow subtraction if they overshoot 20.

DISCUSSION QUESTIONS
● *Which number do you hope will be next? Why?*
● *Can you win with one more throw?*
● *What will you do if you go over 20?*

VARIATION
Begin at 20 (or 30 or 40) and take turns to count back to exactly 0, so the children throw the dice and then keep subtracting the numbers from the figure you began with.

EXTENSIONS
● Allow the children to add or subtract *each throw* in order to get closer to the target total.
● Suggest the children use a polyhedral dice and subtract from 50. The first pair to reach 0 wins. Allow addition if they overshoot.

WHAT CAN YOU BUY FOR 50P?

†† *About ten children sitting in a circle*
🕐 *About 15 minutes*

AIM
To exchange and calculate confidently with coins.

YOU WILL NEED
Counters, cubes or plastic shapes such as bears, enough money to total 50p in mixed coins for each pair, a price list pinned up, for example:

Large bears	12p
Middle-sized bears	10p
Small bears	6p

HOW TO PLAY
Ask each pair to take 50p in mixed coins and to find out as quickly as possible the number of large bears they can buy for 50p. Emphasise that you will need to see the bears, the money and the change in front of them before you say 'Ready', then everyone must stop so you can check what they have done. The first pair to show a correct answer wins a counter. Try other questions such as 'How quickly can you find out how many small bears you can buy with 50p?' Continue until one pair of children has five counters.

DISCUSSION QUESTIONS
● *How many bears did you buy?*
● *How did you work it out?*
● *Can you write a number sentence about it?*
● *How much did all the bears you bought cost?*
● *Did you have any change? How much?*
● *How can we check you have spent the 50p?*
● *Do you think you'll be able to buy more middle-sized bears than large/small bears? Why?*

ASSESSMENT QUESTIONS
● *Are the children making correct exchanges?* Many children, if they need 5p instead of a 10p, will place a 10p in the tray and exchange it for 5p!
● *Do the children realise that all the 50p must be accounted for (there may be change)?*

EXTENSION
Make the bears more expensive and the amount to spend larger. Values such as 20p, 21p and 19p respectively for the bears will encourage compensation with 1p more/less. If the bears cost 21p the children may try five at 20p each, plus five 1ps and realise that you can only buy four or less.

NUMBER SENTENCES

†† *About ten children sitting in a circle*
🕐 *About 10 minutes*

AIM
To recognise, and appreciate the effects of, the operation signs.

YOU WILL NEED
Enough 1–9 cards for each pair to have three cards, subtraction and addition cards, counters.

HOW TO PLAY
Give each pair three number cards and the two sign cards and ask them to make the largest total possible. When they have had sufficient time, ask each pair to read their sentence to the group. The largest correct answer wins a counter. Next ask which pair can make the smallest number using their three cards. Take in and redeal the cards, and repeat until one pair has won five counters.

DISCUSSION QUESTIONS
● *Does the –/+ sign make the answer bigger or smaller?*
● *Gurdeep and Kelly have made 6 (for example, 4 + 3 – 1). What will happen if they swap the sign cards? How else could they rearrange their cards?*

ASSESSMENT QUESTIONS
● *How quickly can the children move the cards?*
● *Do they realise that the two biggest numbers must be totalled and the smallest number subtracted to make the largest number possible?*
● *Have any children used negative numbers?*

EXTENSIONS
● Concentrate on teens or multiples of 10.
● Could the children write a different number sentence to get the same answer?

STRATEGIES

CHILDREN SHOULD BE WORKING WITH NUMBERS OF THE ORDER:

RECEPTION/PRIMARY 1
- counting in 2s using feet, hands and 2p coins;
- sharing objects between 2 (halving) or 3.

YEAR 1/PRIMARY 2
- doubles and halves of numbers to 10 then 20;
- division as both sharing and repeated subtraction.

YEAR 2/PRIMARY 3
- doubles and halves of numbers to 20;
- dividing multiples of 10 by 10, or 40 ÷ 4, or 40 ÷ 10;
- use multiplication facts from 2×, 5× or 10× tables for multiplication and division;
- know that 2 × 10 = 10 × 2 but 10 ÷ 2 is not equal to 2 ÷ 10;
- use multiplication facts to do division where there is a small remainder (5 ÷ 2 = 2r1);
- understand that if they know 3 × 5 = 15, they also know 5 × 3 = 15, 15 ÷ 3 = 5 and 15 ÷ 5 = 3.

AS A MINIMUM BY THE END OF YEAR 2/PRIMARY 3 MOST CHILDREN SHOULD KNOW:

- doubles of numbers to 10 and recognise this as multiplying by 2;
- half of each even number to 20 and recognise this as dividing by 2;
- 2× and 10× multiplication tables and be gaining familiarity with the 5× table;
- about using remainders when dividing;
- the fact that if you know 2 × 8 = 16 then you also know 16 ÷ 8 = 2 and be able to use this inverse.

Many things can slow children down and stop them from developing more efficient and effective strategies. The single most significant is a lack of known facts to draw upon. However, many adults still feel traumatised at being asked to answer 'times tables' questions very quickly as a result of their childhood experiences. These fears are easily passed on to children. Some children may be very anxious about starting multiplication and division, especially those with older siblings who are finding the concept difficult. It is vital that Early Years teachers begin this work in a non-threatening way. Multiplication is a shorter, quicker way of finding the answer to problems involving repeatedly adding on the same amount, so 3 + 3 + 3 + 3 is the same as 4 × 3.

By the time young children move on to acquiring some multiplication facts and exploring the concept of division, they will already recognise that counting on makes numbers larger and that counting back makes numbers smaller. They will be familiar with counting in groups of 2, 5 and 10, particularly through using money, and should be aware that it is quicker to add or subtract in groups rather than in 1s. Many of the children will have started to memorise the patterns involved in such counting.

STRATEGIES FOR MULTIPLICATION

Knowing a range of multiplication facts will facilitate addition, multiplication and division problems. It is important that children develop quick recall of multiplication and division facts.

Acquiring and remembering these facts should be done systematically and should be reinforced by a range of activities which focus on the patterns of multiples involved and the inter-relationships between the various times tables:

All the numbers in the 5 times table have a 0 or a 5 at the end.
Work out the 5× table by halving the 10× table.
Work out 4 × 8 by doubling 2 × 8.
'If I know that two lots of 5 make 10, I also know that five lots of 2 make 10 and that I can share 10 equally between 2 to have 5 each, or half of 10 is 5, or I can divide 10 into 5 lots of 2.'

Multiplication facts are quickly forgotten by many children, so it is vital to use spare moments to rehearse them using shopping tasks, finger play, looking at the patterns on the number line or through a game or, with older children, by having a fact of the day.

Counting in groups will become familiar to the children through counting in 2s, then 10s and 5s, and later 3s and 4s and many children will quickly start to memorise the patterns in counting on and back. Emphasise the efficiency of counting in groups by asking, 'Why are we adding (or subtracting) in groups rather than in 1s?'

Use classroom displays to help reinforce groupings by arranging the children's pictures in groups. These could be labelled:
- How many groups of daffodils?
- How many flowers in each group?
- Can you count them in groups of 5?

Our bodies are very helpful too. Young children sitting round in a circle counting legs, feet and hands soon learn the rhythm of counting on and back in 2s. Similarly, fingers or toes can be used to count on or back in 5s and 10s. Children who find this difficult should be placed near the beginning of the count and helped and encouraged by other children.

Introduce money once the children are confident with counting in this way. Use 2p, 5p and 10p coins. Sit the children in a semicircle and place some 5p coins on the carpet, one at a time, encouraging the children to count in 5s with you. (You may want to stop after five 5s to begin with.) Remove the coins, one at a time, to encourage counting back in 5s.
Ask:
- How many 5p coins?
- How much money is that?

Number patterns are important in developing sets of number facts. Help the children to begin to remember some number patterns: odds and evens, the multiples of 5, the 10s numbers and so on.

Write the numbers on the board and ask:
- Can you see a pattern?
- Can you describe the pattern?
- If you are counting in 5s, which end

numbers would you expect? Would you expect to say 34? Why not?
- Can we say the numbers together using our fingers to match each number?

Learning to count in 5s using fingers enables children to dispense with the traditional chant:
- Five lots of 5 – raise five fingers and try to remember the answer.
- 25 is how many groups of 5? (Count fingers in 5s until the answer is reached. Then ask again who can remember five lots of 5 without counting.)
- Wriggle your fingers, 'Who can show me how many groups of 5 make 25?' Later try ten lots of 5 and ask '50 is how many lots of 5?'

When the children have memorised these, four lots of 5, six lots of 5 and nine lots of 5 can be easily found. You may need to model these together:
- Who can quickly show five lots of 5?
- Who can tell me the answer?
- Fold one finger, how many 5s now?
- Who knows the answer to four lots of 5?
- Can you explain how you found the answer? (You will be encouraging the children to take away 5.)

Go on to use these ideas with 2s and 10s.

STRATEGIES FOR DIVISION

Division can be modelled in two very different ways: sharing and repeated subtraction. It is important to help children become familiar with both models. They will need to learn to share out objects: for example to share eight apples fairly between four people or to share six cubes into two equal piles. They will also need to learn to sort objects into groups by repeated subtraction: for example how many pairs of gloves can they make with 14 gloves? How many jumps of 5 will I need to get to 35 on the number line?

There is a potential difficulty in the fact that we use the same operation sign for these two models of division: sharing between 4 or dividing into 4s. Consider $100 \div 4 = 25$, do I get 25 groups of 4 or have 4 people each received 25 items? Both are examples of division and it is unhelpful and confusing to represent only one model as division. It is important not to rush into formal recording and to work with problems that give children frequent access to both models for division.

ALL THE 10S

ϯϯ *Whole class sitting in a semicircle with the teacher in the space*
🕐 *About 5 minutes*

AIMS
To reinforce the pattern of counting in 10s. To promote fingers as a calculation aid.

WHAT TO DO
Ask the children to imagine that each of their fingers is worth 10. Show them how to fold their fingers in a fist and, as you count together in 10s, lift a finger. Count in 10s together up to 100. Make sure every child is synchronising the words and actions. Practise until the children are confident, and then count back in 10s.

DISCUSSION QUESTIONS
Go on to ask questions such as:
● *Who can show me 30? How many 10s are in that number?*
● *Who can show me 50? How many 10s is that?*
● *How many 10s make 60?*

EXTENSIONS
● Ask the children 'What is five 10s and three more 10s? Who can show me with their fingers? How many 10s is that?'
● Can you work out 60 – 20 using your fingers.

FOUR 5S ARE 20

ϯϯ *Whole class sitting with their legs folded in a circle with the teacher*
🕐 *2–3 minutes*

AIM
To introduce a strategy for counting in 5s up to 20.

WHAT TO DO
You might like to begin by referring to the activity 'Keeping very fit' on page 13 in which the children count up to 20s in 5s and 1s with their hands and feet if they have tried this previously.

Tell the children that today they are going to learn to count in 5s up to 20. Ask them if they know how many toes there are on one foot. Model the counting for the children by putting out one foot and saying 'Five' and then the other foot and saying 'Ten'. Ask the children to join in with you, encouraging them to put out their feet and count 'Five, ten'. Then tell them to fold their legs back one at a time, saying 'Five, nought'.

Then ask, 'Who can put out two 5s? How many toes is that?' Model four 5s by unfolding your legs one at a time, saying 'Five, ten'. Then put out one arm and say 'Fifteen', then the other arm and say 'Twenty'. Fold back your legs and practise together, making sure that the words and actions are synchronised.

DISCUSSION QUESTIONS
● *Can you show me 20? How many 5s is that?*
● *Can you show me 15? How many 5s is that?*
● *Can you show me no 5s? How many is that?*
● *Can you show me three 5s? How many is that?*
● *Can you show me the numbers on the number line? Can we read them together?*

EXTENSIONS
Move on to larger numbers of 5s by counting round the circle all the children's fingers. (So the first child will say '5, 10'; the second child '15, 20'; the third child '25, 30'...). They then count their toes (the same chant as for fingers) and finally their fingers and toes. (The first child will say '5, 10, 15, 20'; the second child: '25, 30, 35, 40': the third child '45, 50'...).
● How many feet will we need for 30? How many lots of 5 is that?
● Have you noticed anything about your first number each time and your last number each time? (The first number always has a 5 in it and the last number always has a 0.)
● Can the children predict who will say which numbers? How do they know? Do they count round in their minds?
Try asking questions such as:
● If we start with Lauren again, who will say 30?
● If we start with Simon, who will say 30 then?
As the children become more confident, encourage them to recite the number sequences without modelling with their hands and feet.

DEVELOPING MENTAL MATHS

MULTIPLICATION AND DIVISION

5P SHOP

✦✦ *About 15 children sitting in a semicircle with the teacher in the space*
🕐 *About 10 minutes*

AIM
To consolidate counting in 5s and to move on to multiplication facts.

YOU WILL NEED
Cubes, counters or plastic counting shapes such as bears, some 5p coins.

WHAT TO DO
Place four items in a line in front of you, for example the plastic bears. Tell the children that the bears cost 5p today and ask them how many 5p coins are needed to buy them. Let one child lay out the coins in front of the bears. Can anyone say how much four 5p coins is? Model the answer by saying, '5, 10, 15, 20p. Four lots of 5 make 20; and 20 is four lots of 5'. Play again, this time laying out a different number of items for the children to count. Note: If the children *know* that four lots of 5 make 20, do not persist in making them count in 5s as this will devalue their higher order knowledge.

DISCUSSION QUESTIONS
● *How do you know we need four 5p coins to buy these bears?*
● *Why are you sure that four 5p coins are worth 20p?*

EXTENSIONS
● Play this game, but change the prices to 2p per bear or 10p for each bear, using coins if appropriate.
● To start to encourage division strategies, label a four-packet of buns '40p'. Show them to the

children and ask them how they can find out how much one bun will cost? Suggestions might be:
● 'There are four 10s in 40, so the buns will cost 10p each';
● 'Forty shared between four is 10 each';
● taking four 10p coins and putting one on each bun.
Model the suggestions with words and apparatus.

HOW MANY 10P COINS IN MY BOX?

✦✦ *About 15 children in a semicircle with the teacher in the space*
🕐 *About 5 minutes*

AIM
To visualise dividing by 10.

YOU WILL NEED
A small box, ten real 10p coins.

WHAT TO DO
Secretly place a number of 10p coins in the box, perhaps five. Tell the children that you have put 50p in your box and ask who can tell you how many ten pence coins that is?

Discuss the various ways they worked it out. Some children may have used fingers to count in 10s up to 50. This is an excellent way of demonstrating the answer and it is worthwhile modelling it with the class. Remove the coins from the box and count them together in 10s, emphasising that five 10s are 50 and so on. Give each child a turn at putting the coins back in the box.

DISCUSSION QUESTIONS
How did you work out how many 10p coins are in the box?

VARIATIONS
Tell the children how many coins are in the box. 'I have four 10p coins, how much is my money worth?'

EXTENSIONS
● After placing the coins in the box, write the number sentence on a large sheet of paper: '60 ÷ 10 = 6' and '6 × 10 = 60'.
● Try the activity using 2p or 5p coins and ask the children to write number sentences.
● For older or more able children, use 20p or 50p coins or mixtures of 20p and 10p coins. Ask questions such as 'I've got five coins that make £1. What are they?'

MULTIPLICATION AND DIVISION

SHARE OUT

†† *About 16 children sitting in pairs on the carpet*
🕐 *About 10 minutes*

AIM
To help children halve even and odd numbers.

YOU WILL NEED
Enough cubes for each pair to take a handful, a large sheet of paper, a thick felt-tipped pen.

WHAT TO DO
Record the names of each pair on the large sheet. Then ask each pair to take a handful of cubes, count them and tell you, in turn, how many they have. Write the numbers next to their names.

Discuss sharing the cubes between each partner and whether the children think this would be fair. Record their answers on the sheet. Then let them share out the cubes and record their answers on the sheet. Circle those answers where the cubes were able to be shared equally and discuss those that weren't. Create two separate lists labelled 'Odd' and 'Even'. Read these together and keep them for later reference.
Note: Older or more able children should be able to do this easily and accurately in their heads for even numbers of 10s such as 20, 40, 60... 100, but may find the odd numbers of 10s harder. This is because they can relate the even numbers of 10s to halving 2, 4, 6... . Although halving even numbers of 10s relates easily to previous knowledge ($\frac{1}{2} \times 4 = 2$, $\frac{1}{2} \times 40 = 20$) children are less likely to have immediate knowledge of halving odd numbers.

DISCUSSION QUESTIONS
● *Before you share your cubes I want you to think if your sharing will be fair? I would like each pair to tell me what they think and why?*
● *Can anyone explain why these numbers shared equally?*
● *Can we read these numbers?*
(Repeat with any odd numbers.)
● *How can we tell if a number is odd or even?*

EXTENSIONS
● Deal out a set of 1–50 cards and work together to sort them into two piles: numbers that will halve exactly and those that will not. Write up the numbers that can be halved exactly with their halves beside them, reminding the children that these are called even numbers. Repeat with the odd numbers, introducing $\frac{1}{2}$s where necessary. (You can introduce the decimal notation for a half): 2... 1; 4... 2; 1... $\frac{1}{2}$; 1... 0.5; 3... $1\frac{1}{2}$... 1.5.

● Go on to try sharing between four (quartering). Tell the pairs to sit in groups of four and to take two handfuls of cubes between them to count together. Record the groups' counts and whether their cubes shared equally between the four of them. Discuss any that did not share equally.

RULER FRACTIONS

†† *Whole class sitting in a semicircle with the teacher in the space*
🕐 *About 5 minutes*

AIM
To encourage the children to visualise fractions through length.

YOU WILL NEED
A metre ruler demarcated into decimetres, two 50cm rulers and four 25cm rulers, or 100cm, 50cm and 25cm strips of card.

WHAT TO DO
Hold up the metre ruler and ask the children if they know how many centimetres long it is. Ask a child to show you where halfway on the ruler is and how many centimetres it is to halfway. Next, compare the 50cm ruler with the metre ruler, and the 25cm ruler with the 50cm, discussing the relationships of their lengths each time. Emphasise that two 50s are 100 and 50 is half of 100, and that two 25s are 50 and 25 is half of 50. Write number sentences together. With older or more able children emphasise that four 25s are 100 and that 25 is $\frac{1}{4}$ of 100. Again, write number sentences together, such as $25 \times 4 = 100$, $100 \div 4 = 25$.

DISCUSSION QUESTIONS
● *How many 50cm rulers will fit along the metre ruler? How do you know? Can you show us?*
● *How many 25cm rulers will fit along the 50cm ruler? How do you know? Come out and show us.*
● *How many 25cm rulers will fit along the metre ruler? (Talk about quarters and dividing by 4.)*

EXTENSION
● Can the children find out what other lengths will fit into a metre. Discuss their methods and results.

DISPLAYING OUR PICTURES

†† *Whole class*
🕐 *About 10 minutes*

AIM
To arrange objects in even-sized groups.

YOU WILL NEED
A suitable-sized display area, small sheets of paper, felt-tipped pen. Recent artwork which the children can display.

WHAT TO DO
Tell the children that you want to pin up their pictures in groups, say, of 5. Point them towards the display area and ask them to try to organise their work appropriately. When they have grouped their work in 5s, ask them to consider the arrangement. Some of the work may need to be overlapped to fit on to the display area. Ask the children for their labelling suggestions: '1 × 5 = 5' or 'One group of five is 5'; '2 × 5 = 10' or 'Two groups of five are 10'; '27 pictures arranged in 5s are 27 ÷ 5 = 5 and 2 left over'; '5 × 5 = 25 and 2 more'. Pin up the pictures in the agreed arrangement, together with captions, and use them as a teaching aid for multiplication and division.

DISCUSSION QUESTIONS
● *How many groups of five are there?*
● *When we arranged two into groups of five why are there two not in a group of five?*
● *If we arranged your work in 10s, would there be more or fewer groups? Can you explain why?*

Would all the pictures be in a group?
● *Is there any way of arranging our pictures so that they can all fit in the same-sized groups?*

VARIATION
Rearrange the pictures into 3s or 4s. Are there still remainders?

TELLING STORIES: 2

†† *Whole class sitting facing the teacher*
🕐 *Each day, up to 5 minutes telling two or three stories*

AIM
To model the maths in stories, focusing on multiplication and division.

WHAT TO DO
Tell the children a number story and ask them to model the numbers with their hands and feet. For example, 'There were four horses in the farmer's field. His daughter gave them each five carrots. How many carrots did she take to the field?' With the children's help, write the appropriate number sentence on the board: 4 × 5 = 20.

Encourage the children to be aware that division is the inverse of multiplication by asking, 'If the farmer's daughter has 20 carrots altogether and she gives each of the four horses the same number of carrots, how many carrots can she give each horse?'

As the children become more confident with bigger numbers make the stories more complicated. Extend the activity by increasing the size of the numbers gradually. Use Base 10 longs and unit cubes to demonstrate these larger numbers. Encourage the children to apply the strategies they have learned for smaller numbers and to use these for solving problems using bigger numbers.

Note: It is important to vary the position of the unknown quantity: ? × 2 = 10 or 10 ÷ ? = 5.

DISCUSSION QUESTIONS
● *What number sentence could we write to tell this story?*
● *If we know that 4 × 5 = 20, what else do we know?*
● *Who can tell us a story to go with this number sentence? (Write on the board: 3 × 3 = 9.)*

ASSESSMENT
Tell the children to put their hands behind their backs. Then tell a more involved story which they must keep track of without looking at their hands.

MULTIPLICATION AND DIVISION

MULTIPLICATION AND DIVISION

ARE YOU 'ODD' OR 'EVEN'?

✚✚ *Whole class in a big space. Great fun at the end of a PE lesson!*
🕐 *About 10 minutes*

AIM
To investigate how many ways a number can be divided exactly.

YOU WILL NEED
A large area, such as the hall or playground, a PE mat, a copy of photocopiable page 64 for each child (optional).

WHAT TO DO
Ask all the children to sit on the floor in a circle. Ask them how they can find out how many children there are in the class today?

Suggest that they each find a partner and sit in a space. If they cannot find a partner, they should sit on the mat. Find out how many groups of two there are by asking the children to stand up and then sit down as you count them. 'Today we have 15 groups of two. 15 groups of two are 30'.

Now tell the children to quickly get into groups of three and sit down. Before they move, ask them to predict if there will be more or less groups and if there will be anyone not in a group. Any 'spare' children should sit on the mat.

Continue making different-sized groups up to 10. You may like to ask the children to make two-equal sized groups – if you can bear it!

Reflect on this investigation back in the classroom by using the writing frame on photocopiable page 64.

DISCUSSION QUESTIONS
● *Will we have more groups of three than we had groups of two, or fewer groups? How do you know?*
● *Will anyone not be in a group? How do you know?*
● *How many will there be if we are all in one group? (The size of the class.)*

EXTENSIONS
● Using a chalkboard or flip chart write up the appropriate number sentences each time. For example:
$30 \div 2 = 15$ and $15 \times 2 = 30$;
$30 \div 3 = 10$ and $10 \times 3 = 30$;
$30 \div 4 = 7r2$ and $4 \times 7 = 28$, $28 + 2 = 30$.
● Point to one of the number sentences (for example, $30 \div 3 = 10$) and ask a child to describe how the class could show you that arrangement (in this case, 'by getting into groups of three'). Encourage the class to do what has been suggested to check if the child is correct.

CAN YOU MAKE A RECTANGLE?

✚✚ *About ten children working in pairs*
🕐 *About 10 minutes*

AIM
To explore making rectangular arrays.

YOU WILL NEED
The same number of squares of card or Multilink for each pair (for example 24), paper, pencils, a copy of photocopiable page 64 for each child (optional).

WHAT TO DO
Organise the children into pairs and give each pair their squares of card (or Multilink). Ask each pair to use their cards to make a rectangle. Choose one rectangle and discuss the number of rows and the number in each row, for example, 'Six rows of 4 are 24'. Turn the rectangle a quarter turn and discuss the same points to show that the answer will remain the same. 'Four rows of 6 are 24'.

Write out the appropriate number sentences so that the children can all see them: $6 \times 4 = 24$, $4 \times 6 = 24$. Explain that 6 and 4 are factors of 24.

52

FINDING HALF

†† *About 10 children working in pairs*
⏱ *About 15 minutes*

AIM
To understand that half can be arranged non-symmetrically.

YOU WILL NEED
Squared paper (enough for each pair), coloured pencils, a copy of photocopiable page 64 for each child (optional).

WHAT TO DO
Arrange the children into pairs and give each pair a sheet of squared paper. Ask the children to draw a box that encloses 12 squares. Then tell

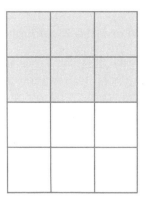

Now ask the children to find out how many different rectangles they can make with the same set of squares and to record their various ways on their pieces of paper. (You may like to give them squared paper on which to record the different ways of arranging the squares.)

Let each pair demonstrate a way of arranging the squares. Observe the various methods. Has anyone tried, for example, one row of 24? How many and what are the factors of 24? They can record their ideas on the writing frame on photocopiable page 64 if you wish.

DISCUSSION QUESTIONS
● *In how many ways can we arrange 24 cards? How can we work systematically?*
● *Which way makes the longest/shortest rows?*
● *I have 4 rows of six chairs, how many chairs do I have altogether?*

EXTENSION
Discuss 'dividing' the cards and write the appropriate number sentences this time: 'I can also see that if I have 24 chairs and I keep making rows of 6 chairs there will be four in each', so 24 ÷ 6 = 4 (and 24 ÷ 4 = 6).

VARIATIONS
● Investigate different numbers. Find out which numbers have the most/least factors (shown by the number of different arrangements possible). Encourage the children to write all the possible number sentences to describe each arrangement of each number of squares.
● Investigate the factors of doubles of a number, for instance the factors of 6, 12, 24, 48, and so on.

them each to take a different-coloured pencil and colour in half the number of squares in their shape.

Encourage them to try enclosing another 12 squares in the same way, but this time to colour in the halves in a different way. This is a good activity to follow-up with the writing frame on photocopiable page 64.

With older children, write number sentences to describe the colouring and show that the halves can be described in the same way each time even though they might look different. You may need to introduce the half symbol.

DISCUSSION QUESTIONS
Ask the children to place all their different patterns in the middle of the table:
● *How many squares have you coloured in each colour?*
● *Have you coloured in the same number of squares each time?*
● *Do all the shapes have $\frac{1}{2}$ the squares coloured in one colour and $\frac{1}{2}$ in another? How can you be sure?*
● *Are all our coloured halves squares or oblongs?*
● *Can we enclose 12 squares in different shapes?*

● *Do our coloured squares need to be next to one another?*
● *What fraction of all the squares on the table are coloured in?*

Beware, children sometimes take this activity to mean colouring half of each small square. This offers a whole extra set of discussion points about the maths language, what you intended the children to do and how they are going to find out how many whole squares they have coloured with each pen: 12 half squares = $\frac{1}{2}$ of 12.

HOW MANY CAN YOU BUY FOR 25P?

†† *About 16 children working in pairs*
⊙ *About 5 minutes*

AIM
To investigate how to buy more than one object.

YOU WILL NEED
Counters, cubes, items from the class shop or plastic counting shapes such as bears, a supply of money, a copy of photocopiable page 64 for each child (optional).

WHAT TO DO
Ask the children to find a partner. Tell them that the cubes cost 5p each today and ask how many they can buy for 25p? Leave them to work in their pairs for a while, but tell them that you will be asking some pairs to explain how they solved the problem. Watch the children carefully to assess their confidence and the strategies that were used. Then ask some pairs to model their answers.

Give the children another problem. (This may be a good opportunity to change the members of some groups.) Tell them that the cubes are more expensive now. They cost 6p, but you still only have 25p. Do the children think they will be able to buy more cubes, fewer cubes or the same amount?

Let them find out. Then discuss their answers and strategies. You may like them to fill in the writing frame on photocopiable page 64 to help them to reflect on their work. Some children may put out coins for each item and add them up and see how much is left; others may be able to calculate mentally.

DISCUSSION QUESTIONS
● *Did you guess correctly whether you would get more for your money?*
● *Can you explain your ideas?*
● *Does anyone have a different idea? Can you explain this new idea?*
● *Can you find other ways to work it out?*

EXTENSIONS
● Try other prices for the cubes from 1p to 25p.
● To develop related division strategies, try these questions. 'If I had 32p, how many cubes could I buy? How much money would I have left over?' or 'I've got 35p. How much more do I need to buy nine boxes? How do you know?'
● Encourage the children to write number sentences to reflect what they have found and tell 'shopping' stories that explain them. For example, 25 ÷ 6 = 4r1, so 'Teddy bears cost 3p and I had 25p, so I could buy four and get 1p change (or had 1p left over)'.

LAST TO STAY STANDING

†† *Whole class standing in a large circle*
🕐 *About 5 minutes*

AIM
To recognise patterns in counting.

HOW TO PLAY
This game can be played with any (counting) pattern, for example multiples of 5.

Count round in the circle '1, 2, 3, 4...'. The child who says 'Five' must sit down. Continue going round and round the circle. Any child who is a multiple of 5 has to sit down until only one child is left standing. This child is the winner.

DISCUSSION QUESTIONS
● *Can you tell yet who will be the last person to be standing?*
● *If we start with Maria, who will have to sit down in the first round?*

VARIATION
Everyone crouches down and whispers '1, 2, 3, 4' and then jumps up, shouting together '5!'. This continues for all the following multiples of five. (This game is great fun, but it may be wise to set a finishing number before you begin, especially if the children are getting excited!)

FIND THE 5S

†† *Four players sitting round a table*
🕐 *About 10 minutes*

AIM
To develop quick recall of multiples of 5.

YOU WILL NEED
A set of cards numbered from 1–50 for each set of four.

HOW TO PLAY
Shuffle the number cards and place them face down in a pile on the table. The children then take turns to pick up a card. If the card is a 0-number or a multiple of 5 it can be kept, but the child must be able to count in 5s up to that number or, as they become more confident, say how many 5s it is. 'My card is 25, that is five 5s'. Otherwise the card is placed on a face-up discard pile. The winner is the child who has collected the most cards when they have all been turned face-up.

DISCUSSION QUESTIONS
● *How do you know which pile to put your card in? How do you know that 32 is not a multiple of 5? How do you know that 40 is a multiple of 5?*
● *How many winning cards are in the 1-50 set?*

VARIATION
Try playing with multiples of 10, or 2 or 3.

EXTENSIONS
● The children can use more than one rule simultaneously in order to claim the card, such as keeping the card if it is a multiple of 2 or 5.
● Use cards up to 100.

HALVING THE 10S

†† *Groups of four children*
🕐 *About 10 minutes*

AIM
To understand that all multiples of 10 are even and therefore can be halved.

YOU WILL NEED
Enough sets of cards numbered 0, 10, 20, 30... 100 for each child in every group of four to receive three cards, a supply of (real) 5p and 10p coins.

HOW TO PLAY
Shuffle the cards and deal out three cards to each group member. Tell them that they must show with their coins half the amount on each of their cards. The winner is the first person to put half the amount on each of their cards. Encourage the use of the words 'odd' and 'even'.

You may need to demonstrate this. Take a card, for instance, 30. Say 'I wonder which coins I will need to show half of 30? Can anyone tell me?' If there are no responses, try asking 'Who knows half of 10? What about half of 20? Now have another think? What about half of 30? Yes, 15. How can I show 15 with the fewest coins? Yes, 10p and 5p.'

DISCUSSION QUESTIONS
● *Which numbers used only 10p coins?*
● *Which numbers used 10p and 5p coins?*
● *Can we arrange them beginning with 10? (Eg, Half of 10 is 5p; Half of 20 is 10p; and so on.)*
● *Can you see a pattern? Can we make up a general rule about this? (If there is an odd number of 10p coins, you will need to use 5p coins to show half of it.)*

ASSESSMENT
What would I get if I had double 25p, or 15p.

MULTIPLICATION AND DIVISION

STRATEGIES

CHILDREN SHOULD BE WORKING WITH NUMBERS OF THE ORDER:

as given on pages 10–11 for counting and ordering, 30–31 for addition and subtraction and 46–47 for multiplication and division.

AS A MINIMUM, BY THE END OF YEAR 2/PRIMARY 3 MOST CHILDREN SHOULD KNOW:

● the effect on numbers of each of the operations and know, for example, that $2 \times 14 = 16$ cannot possibly be right;
● it is quicker to multiply to solve $3 + 3 + 3 + 3 + 3 = ?$;
● to work out how many 2s in 14 it is quicker to divide than to use repeated subtraction;
● know that $13 + 6 = 6 + 13$ but that $13 \div 6$ is not equal to $6 \div 13$;
● know that $12 \times 2 = 2 \times 12$ but that $12 \div 2$ is not equal to $2 \div 12$.

Further detail is given on the pages listed above.

There are many situations in maths where several different number operations might be required to solve a problem. Children need to consider which one is the best for each situation.

In the classroom, there are often mathematical problems that the children can help to solve. They will probably suggest a variety of methods for reaching the solution, giving lots of opportunities for discussion of which is the simplest/most efficient strategy and how to be systematic.

Consider, for example:

● *How can we find out how much money has been collected?*

The children might suggest sorting the coins into their different values; counting in the different values and adding the separate totals together; making £1 piles of mixed coins. You can then ask questions such as: 'How many 10p coins do you need to make £1? How many 5p coins? How do you know?'

To solve the problem the children have been counting in groups, adding single- and two-digit numbers and/or multiplying by the coin values and then dividing or using repeated subtraction to answer your further questions.

● *How many coaches will we need to order to take 100 children to the zoo?*

Encourage the children to consider how many seats there are on a coach and whether all coaches have the same number of seats. Discuss whether 'Two and a half coaches', or 'Two coaches and 16 children can't go!' are acceptable answers. The problem will involve division or repeated subtraction, but more importantly, the discussion will focus on the reasonableness of an answer.

● *Consider planning a school party.*

There is plenty of maths to consider in this situation, with a variety of ways of reaching the answers to discuss. How many children will there be? So how many tables do we need? What will we eat and how much of each food or drink will we need? How much will it cost each child?

Estimating first should be encouraged when children are presented with a new problem and then considering the steps they will need to take. It is possible that there will be more than one way to solve the problem and it is valuable to discuss the fact that neither is wrong (although one might be quicker).

Transforming problems into number sentences that indicate an answer 'at the end' is a common adult strategy – but this process of transformation is difficult and often far from clear to children.

> Consider this rather simple problem: At the start of playtime Jenny had 17 stickers. Her friend gave her some more and now she has 23 stickers. How many stickers did Jenny's friend give her?

Many adults will represent this as 23 – 17 = ?, transforming the problem directly into the number sentence needed to answer it. This does not reflect, however, the narrative sense of the problem. This narrative sense might be better reflected in an open number sentence (one where the unknown quantity is not at the end) such as: 17 + ? = 23. This second option is more useful to pupils learning to tackle this type of problem. It is more likely to fit with their understanding of the problem.

Children's access to problems and open number sentences (where the unknown is not at the end) is often restricted because adults feel that these are more difficult. Research* indicates that where children are taught to read and use all number sentence types then they are more successful at solving problems.

The range of problems that need consideration might be represented by the following expressions (as well as multistep number operations using brackets). You may like to explore with the children examples such as:

? + 6 = 9	14 + ? = 21	5 + ? = 12
? – ? = 9	? – 7 = 14	15 – 3 = ?
3 × ? = 9	7 × ? = 21	2 × 6 = ?
27 ? 3 = 9	21 ÷ ? = 3	12 ÷ 6 = ?

Writing stories or problems to illustrate number sentences, as well as encouraging children to write number sentences to reflect problems, will help them to develop confidence with the full range of possibilities listed above.

* Carpenter, TJ, Moser, JM and Bebout, H (1988) 'Representation of addition and subtraction word problems' in *Journal for Research in Mathematics Education*, 19/4/345–57.

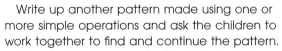

Write up another pattern made using one or more simple operations and ask the children to work together to find and continue the pattern.

This would be an excellent activity to follow-up by using the writing frame on photocopiable page 64 for the children to record their work.

VARIATIONS
● Work on sequences that change regularly:
+3: 3, 6, 9...
×2: 5, 10, 20, 40...
−4: 31, 27, 23, 19...
● Draw up a string of 'number beads' giving the operations and asking the children to write up the numbers, for example:

● Try a pattern that begins at the higher number and descends, for example:

EXTENSION
Give the children two numbers. What could the third be? What is the rule? For example, 4 and 6 → 8, where the rule is +2; or 10, where the rule is '× 2 − 2'. The children could make up sequences and problems of this kind to swap with their friends.

KEEP ON GOING

†† *About 15 children sitting facing the chalkboard/flip chart*
🕐 *About 10 minutes*

AIM
To develop strategies for exploring and continuing a pattern.

YOU WILL NEED
A sequence written on the chalkboard/flip chart with the blanks indicated (see the caterpillar below), a copy of photocopiable page 64 for each child (optional).

WHAT TO DO
Ask the children to look at the numbers carefully and to try to explain what is happening to them. They may note that some of the numbers are getting bigger and some are getting smaller.

Encourage them to look at the differences between the numbers to see if they can observe a pattern. What is the pattern? (The numbers get 6 bigger then 3 smaller.) Ask them to check to see if they have found the pattern by filling in the blanks – who knows what might come next? Continue until the pattern is complete.

FINDING THE TOTAL

†† *Children working in pairs*
🕐 *10 minutes, then a further 15 minutes for investigation*

AIM
To investigate number combinations.

YOU WILL NEED
Paper, pencils, counting apparatus, photocopiable page 62, photocopiable page 64 one for each child (optional).

WHAT TO DO
Draw a target on the board, as shown opposite or using different numbers.

Choose a total for which the children can aim, for example 12. Tell them that they can use any three of the numbers on the target to reach this chosen number. They can also use the same number more than once if they wish. Start the children off with a few examples of suitable addition triples. Write down their suggestions: 4 + 4 + 4 = 12; 6 + 5 + 1 = 12; 7 + 3 + 2 = 12 and so on. Give them about 10 minutes to work on the problem before bringing them together to list all their ideas. If they have not done so, work together to sort the children's number sentences into 'a pattern' to encourage them to be systematic.

Go on to ask if they can make 12 using any other signs and operations. For example: 2 × 5 + 2 = 12 or 5 × 1 + 7 = 12 or 3 × 5 − 3 = 12.

This would be an excellent activity to follow-up by using the writing frame on photocopiable page 64 on which the children can record and reflect on their work.

DISCUSSION QUESTIONS
● *Can anyone suggest which numbers I can add to make the number 12? What if I can use other operations?*
● *How many different number sentences can you write for the target number?*

VARIATION
Give each pair a copy of photocopiable page 64, two red counters and one yellow one. Tell the children to move the counters around to cover three numbers to make the chosen number, but explain that numbers covered by a red counter must be added and the number covered by the yellow counter must be taken away. How many

ways can they find to make the chosen number? Make this more challenging by specifying that multiplication and subtraction only, for example, can be used.

EXTENSION
Let the children use four numbers, but say that they must use at least two different operations to reach the chosen number.

CAN YOU MAKE THEM BALANCE?

†† *Whole class*
🕐 *About 30 minutes*

AIM
To investigate how different number operations can be used to achieve the same answer.

YOU WILL NEED
Chalkboard, counting apparatus, paper, pencils, calculators, photocopiable page 64, one for each child (optional).

WHAT TO DO
Draw this balance on the board.

Ask the children to look at the picture, and choose a child to read the sum in the first bucket. Then ask them for the answer. Encourage one of the children to come out to write the answer in the 'balance' in the middle.

Now ask the children to think of some numbers and signs to make 'sums' that will balance with 3 and could be written in the right-hand bucket. Share ideas: 8 − 5; 10 − 7; 13 − 10; 1 + 2; 0 + 3; 2 + 1; 6 ÷ 2 and so on. Write them around the bucket and check together. It is important for the children to realise that there may be several ways of solving a problem.

Ask the children to work in pairs to try to find other number sentences. After ten minutes check their ideas, making sure everyone has a turn. Observe how many different sentences they have discovered.

Choose a number sentence together to write on a second balance and leave the children to look for suitable number sentences to balance it. You may like to give each pair a personal challenge with a number sentence suitable for their ability. This activity could be followed-up with photocopiable page 64 for the children to reflect on their work.

EXTENSION

● Give the children a total and encourage them to devise some problems for themselves using different operations on each side of the balance.
● Make the activity even more demanding by asking for three different number sentences each with a different operation, or ask for sentences with more than one operation: 24 – 10 = 14, 7 × 2 = 14, 28 ÷ 2 = 14, or 2 × 5 + 4 = 14. For larger answers (numbers with lots of factors, such as 24), ask the children to only use one operation, such as multiplication, and look at the different ways of getting the same answer.

VARIATION

Very young children can explore using just one operation.

HOW MUCH MONEY WILL I HAVE?

✝ *About 15 children, arranged in groups of 2, 3 or 4*
⏲ *About 5 minutes*

AIM

To investigate how the same amount can be divided in different ways.

YOU WILL NEED

A supply of money, a copy of photocopiable page 64 for each child (optional).

WHAT TO DO

Write a problem on the board, such as:

> Granny has sent you 50p (or £5 or £50) for Christmas.
> How much money will each person in your group receive?

Tell the children that when you see that the money has been divided you will be asking the members of the groups how much they received. Explain that they do not necessarily have to divide the money equally, though you may like to specify this. However, if they do try to share equally, some groups may have to decide what to do with the remainder.

This is an excellent activity for assessment. You will be able to see how the children exchange coins and how they explain remainders.

Rearrange the children so that they are each in a different-sized group and repeat the activity. You

may find it valuable for the children to complete the writing frame or photocopiable page 64 in which the children can write about the effect of different groupings on the maths.

DISCUSSION QUESTIONS

Ask each group:
● *How did you solve the problem?*
● *How much did each child in your group receive?*
● *Was there any money left over? How much?*
● *Which size group would you like to be in? Why?*

VARIATION

Ask the children to suggest an amount of money to share, for example £100.

EVERY NUMBER UP TO 20

✝ *About 10 children in pairs*
⏲ *About 10 minutes, then 10 minutes discussion*

AIMS

To investigate making all the numbers from 1 to 20 using 1, 2, 3, 4 and 5. (Make the numbers from 1 to 10 for younger children.) To investigate how to use different number operations to solve problems.

YOU WILL NEED

Sets of cards numbered 1, 2, 3, 4 and 5 and several cards with the four operations signs written on them (enough for each pair), paper, pencils, a copy of photocopiable page 64 for each child (optional), chalkboard.

MULTISTEP AND MIXED OPERATIONS

WHAT TO DO

Ask the children to sit looking at the chalkboard. Lay out the cards and ask for a volunteer to arrange the cards and signs to make a number sentence where the answer is 3. Possible suggestions might include: 1 + 2; 4 – 1; 1 + 1 + 1; 4 + 4 – 3.

Then set the children to work in pairs. Give each pair a set of cards to help them and explain that you would like them to make all the numbers from 1 to 20 (or 1 to 10 for younger or less able children). Give them paper and pencils and ask them to record their ideas as they go along.

After about 10 minutes work, bring the class together, facing the board again and ask who can write a number sentence to make 10. Answers may include 4 + 4 + 2; 3 × 3 + 1 and so on. Go on to ask who can write number sentences to give the answer 9. For example: 4 + 4 + 1; 3 × 3; 2 × 4 +1. Give praise particularly to children who are being adventurous with number operations. Continue for all the numbers.

Follow-up with the writing frame on photocopiable page 64.

DISCUSSION QUESTIONS

● *How can you work systematically?*
● *How can you use trial and improvement?*
● *If you have made 8 with 2 × 4, how can you use that to get 7? (2 × 4 – 1.)*

EXTENSION

Limit the children to using each of the numbers only once in any number sentence. Can they still make all the numbers to 20?

VARIATION

Choose a number suitable for the children, such as 10. Tell them that someone has written this number in his or her book as the answer to a maths

problem. What do the children think the question might have been? Still working in their pairs, ask them to write down some of their ideas. After ten minutes ask each pair for their suggestions. Less confident children should be asked first.

Record the children's answers on the board. If you are using 10, begin with the addition bonds to 10. Ask the children to help you rearrange the bonds into a pattern (0 and 10, 1and 9 and so on). Continue until all the combinations have been used. Move on to subtraction bonds, then multiplication and division sentences.

WHAT HAPPENS?

†† *About 16 children sitting in pairs on the carpet*
🕐 *About 10 minutes*

AIM

To investigate what happens when we operate with odd and even numbers.

YOU WILL NEED

Two dice, a red and a blue pencil crayon (for each pair), paper, calculators, a copy of photocopiable page 64 for each child (optional).

WHAT TO DO

Ask the children to take turns in their pairs to throw both dice and to write the sum of the two numbers they get. Tell them that every odd number should be written in red and every even number in blue.

After ten minutes, ask the children to gather around the board to share their ideas. Write their answers on the board, using one colour for odd numbers and one for even numbers.

Let the children investigate, either now or in another session, subtracting odd and even numbers and then multiplying and dividing them. Offer calculators to help with the multiplication and division problems.

Ask the children to record their thoughts and ideas by using the writing frame on photocopiable page 64.

DISCUSSION QUESTIONS

● *Have you noticed anything?*
● *Who can explain what has happened?*
● *Can we write a general rule for adding odd and even numbers?*
● *What about subtracting or multiplying and dividing odds and evens? Is there a general rule? Is it easier or harder than for adding? Why do you say that?*

DEVELOPING MENTAL MATHS

TARGET

DEVELOPING MENTAL MATHS

DOGGY FRACTIONS

DEVELOPING MENTAL MATHS

MENTAL MATHS WRITING FRAME

The activity was about: _____

The easy parts were:_____

They were easy because: _____

_____

How did you solve the problem? Tick a box.
Did you:

☐ ask another pupil?   ☐ use apparatus?

☐ ask an adult?   ☐ think long and hard
by yourself?

Which apparatus did
you use? Write or
draw a picture.

Do you enjoy solving
maths problems?
Colour in a face.

😊 😐 ☹️

Draw a picture of how
you solved this
problem. You could
use a 'thinking' bubble
to show how you did
things in your head.

DEVELOPING MENTAL MATHS